MICROSOFT® EXCEL 97
QUICK REFERENCE

MICROSOFT®
EXCEL 97
QUICK REFERENCE

by Joyce J. Nielsen

Microsoft® Excel 97 Quick Reference

Copyright© 1997 by Que® Corporation.

Library of Congress Catalog No.: 97-65032

ISBN: 0-7897-1165-6

99 98 97   6 5 4 3 2 1

Interpretation of the printing code: the rightmost double-digit number is the year of the book's printing; the rightmost single-digit number, the number of the book's printing. For example, a printing code of 97-1 shows that the first printing of the book occurred in 1997.

Credits

PRESIDENT
Roland Elgey

PUBLISHER
Joseph B. Wikert

PUBLISHING DIRECTOR
David W. Solomon

ACQUISITIONS MANAGER
Elizabeth South

EDITORIAL SERVICES DIRECTOR
Elizabeth Keaffaber

MANAGING EDITOR
Michael Cunningham

DIRECTOR OF MARKETING
Lynn E. Zingraf

ACQUISITIONS EDITOR
Angela Wethington

PRODUCT DIRECTOR
Carolyn Kiefer

PRODUCTION EDITOR
Lori A. Lyons

EDITOR
Christine Prakel

STRATEGIC MARKETING MANAGER
Barry Pruett

PRODUCT MARKETING MANAGER
Kris Ankney

ASSISTANT PRODUCT MARKETING MANAGERS
Karen Hagen
Christy M. Miller

TECHNICAL EDITOR
Noel Fields

TECHNICAL SUPPORT SPECIALIST
Nadeem Muhammed

ACQUISITIONS COORDINATOR
Tracy M. Williams

EDITORIAL ASSISTANT
Virginia Stoller

BOOK DESIGNER
Ruth Harvey

COVER DESIGNER
Dan Armstrong

PRODUCTION TEAM
Michelle Croninger
Toi Davis
Stephanie Hammett
Debbie Kincaid
Joy Dean Lee
Candyce McCreary
Terri Sheehan
Karen Teo
Holly Wittenberg

INDEXER
Sandy Henselmeier
Nadia Ibrahim
Tim Taylor

Composed in *Century Old Style* and *Franklin Gothic* by Que Corporation.

About the Author

Joyce J. Nielsen is an independent computer consultant, specializing in writing and developing books based on microcomputer software applications. Prior to her work as a consultant, Joyce was a Senior Product Development Specialist for Que Corporation. She is the author or co-author of over 20 computer books, including Que's *Special Edition Using 1-2-3 97 for Windows 95, Microsoft Office 97 Quick Reference,* and *Word for Windows 95 Visual Quick Reference.* Nielsen also worked as a Research Analyst for a shopping mall developer, where she developed and documented computer applications used nationwide. She received a Bachelor of Science degree in Quantitative Business Analysis from Indiana University. You may contact her via CompuServe at 76507,2712 or via the Internet at **jnielsen@iquest.net.**

Acknowledgments

Microsoft Excel 97 Quick Reference is the result of the efforts of many talented and dedicated people. I would like to thank the following people in particular for their numerous contributions to this book: David Solomon, Angie Wethington, Lisa Wagner, Carolyn Kiefer, Lori Lyons, Noel Fields, and Christine Prakel.

We'd Like to Hear from You!

As part of our continuing effort to produce books of the highest possible quality, Que would like to hear your comments. To stay competitive, we *really* want you, as a computer book reader and user, to let us know what you like or dislike most about this book or other Que products.

You can mail comments, ideas, or suggestions for improving future editions to the address below, or send us a fax at (317) 581-4663. For the online inclined, Macmillan Computer Publishing has a forum on CompuServe (type **GO QUEBOOKS** at any prompt) through which our staff and authors are available for questions and comments. The address of our Internet site is **http://www.mcp.com** (World Wide Web).

In addition to exploring our forum, please feel free to contact me personally to discuss your opinions of this book: I'm **104521,2411** on CompuServe, and I'm **ckiefer@que.mcp.com** on the Internet.

Thanks in advance—your comments will help us to continue publishing the best books available on computer topics in today's market.

Carolyn Kiefer
Product Development Specialist
Que Corporation
201 W. 103rd Street
Indianapolis, Indiana 46290
USA

Table of Contents

Charts and Graphics 29

Customizing   59

Editing Workbooks

File Management 137

Formatting 155

Formula & Function Management 173

Functions Mini-Reference 211

Introduction

The *Microsoft Excel 97 Quick Reference* is the latest in a series of comprehensive, task-oriented references and details how to use the features and functionality of Excel 97. Compiled for the intermediate-to-advanced user who wants a concise, comprehensive reference, the *Microsoft Excel 97 Quick Reference* is loaded with detailed instructions outlining important tasks you need to complete.

The *Microsoft Excel 97 Quick Reference* presents the tasks and functions most often sought by users of Excel 97. This book also includes a comprehensive glossary with many terms and definitions that refer to the newest features in Excel 97.

New Ways of Working

Que's Quick References help the reader cover the most ground with the least amount of hassle, in a minimum of time! Tasks include steps that the reader can complete—usually no more than five steps to any task.

The goal of the author is to help you get your work done in the least amount of time, with a minimum of reading and learning. The author knows that your time is valuable, and that you may not need to use some of the included tasks very often. That's why each task in this book is written with economy in mind. The reader should be able to recognize a need, take this book off the shelf, and complete a task within minutes; then put the book back on the shelf for future reference. It just doesn't get any faster or easier.

Expanded Coverage

Unlike other low-cost references, Que's *Microsoft Excel 97 Quick Reference* covers every major functional element of Excel 97. More importantly, each element is covered separately, in its own dedicated section in this book. You can be confident that this book covers a lot of ground. The *Microsoft Excel 97 Quick Reference* even includes a reference to Excel functions that are the most useful.

Who Should Read This Book?

The *Microsoft Excel 97 Quick Reference* is written for casual to advanced computer users who need a fast reference to Excel 97 tasks, functions, and features. It is an ideal companion to Que's *Special Edition Using Microsoft Excel 97*. The Quick Reference size makes it ideal for travel.

If you are upgrading from Excel 95 or Excel 5, you will find this reference useful for finding new features and looking up new ways of getting a job done. If you are migrating from another spreadsheet program, such as Lotus 1-2-3, this Quick Reference may be the right amount of instruction you need to transfer your know-how investment to new products.

As a reference, this book is not intended to tutor learners. If you are just starting to use Excel software for the first time, or are a very casual user, you may want to consider Que's *User Friendly Using Microsoft Excel 97* or *The Complete Idiot's Guide to Microsoft Excel 97* as a book to get you up to speed. For beginner or very casual task reference, check out Que's *Easy Microsoft Excel 97*. If you want the most complete reference as well as tutorial and foundation information, then you need Que's *Special Edition Using Microsoft Excel 97*. This *Microsoft Excel 97 Quick Reference* makes an ideal companion to the comprehensive Special Edition.

Features of the *Excel 97 Quick Reference*

If you take a moment to glance over the table of contents, you'll note that each logical part of the Excel 97 product has its own dedicated section in this book. Topics are organized into working groups under each logical part of Excel, with related tasks sorted under each topic in alphabetical order. In some cases, tasks have been specially sorted by the author when task grouping, sequencing, or relationships indicate the order.

Content Tuned to Your Needs

You can't be expected to know everything; and yet, you don't have to be told everything either. That's why the Quick Reference author has been given wide latitude in determining what extra information you might find valuable to complete a task. By tuning the presentation to your needs, you can spend less time sifting through background information or cross-referencing related information just to be sure you're using a task appropriately. For example, the author often indicates which *conditions* must exist in order to complete a task. The author explains why one task is best to use over another—all in very succinct text. Where it is obvious to you what conditions must exist or which task is best, you won't be slowed by text telling you what you already know.

Expert Advice

Our expert author knows when a specific task is appropriate and when that task should be avoided. For example, there is no point in making a bulleted list if only one list item exists. This book tells you when a task is in order, and when you should avoid using a task when it's out of context or is not appropriate at a specific location in your document, database, or presentation. This expertise of the author transfers directly to your work through this approach.

Navigation and Steps

Author expertise can also help keep tasks simple by including or eliminating steps that guide you to where you enter information or perform an action. Tasks in this book that do detail how to get where you're going do so because the author believes that getting there is confusing for the reader.

In other cases, where your starting point is not relevant or where you are likely to know where a menu or dialog is located, the author keeps it simple by not adding the navigational detail. The same assumptions apply where individual actions can be compounded into a step. Beginners often need "baby steps" to avoid confusion. The need for such care soon passes for most, and the user is better able to work with a step that is a logical group of actions. The result is a more readable set of steps.

The author has limited the length of commands and steps to just the words you need to read to complete each task in a minimum of time. Intermediate users of Windows-based applications rarely need to be told when to click the OK button!

Expert Mentoring

You also get background information, when appropriate, to the topic or task. Tasks are often introduced so that your understanding of the real purpose of the task is clarified. Although mentoring is best done through the full *Special Edition Using* series, there are times when a little mentoring before a task greatly enhances the understanding of that task or function. The author keeps this in mind while using her extensive user experience to determine when to provide that reinforcing conceptual information.

A Comprehensive Glossary

With the Internet awareness of the Microsoft Excel 97 product comes a lot of jargon that will be new to you. This book has a glossary of terms specific to who you are and what you're doing. These terms are contained in various sections of the book as italicized words. Look them up as you go along or scan for any terms that may not be familiar. Ever wonder what *concatenation* is? You don't have to complete a task to find out. You can check out such terms or definitions in the glossary.

Task Reference

This Quick Reference is divided into sections, all dedicated to Excel 97 functional areas. In each section, you will find an alphabetical listing of topics that are detailed with tasks.

To find all tasks that cover printing, for example, go to the "Outputting" section, find the task topic "Printing," and then turn to the tasks that cover activities in that topic area. Tasks follow one another and are sorted in alphabetical order, unless there is special value in completing multiple tasks in order.

When a prerequisite task must be read to understand the task you are reading, a cross reference will let you know: (See "Page Setup: Setting a Print Area" before you complete this task.). When other tasks may be more useful, or may be used instead of the task you are viewing, a cross reference will let you know where to find it: (See also "Alignment: Shrinking Text to Fit in a Cell" in the Formatting section.) And when other related tasks may be useful after completing a task, a cross reference at the end of the task will direct you to their location: (See also "Internet: Browsing Web Files," "Internet: Creating Hyperlinks," and "Internet: Getting Data from a Web Site.")

Conventions Used in This Book

This book uses certain conventions in order to guide you through the various tasks. Special typefaces in this Quick Reference include the following:

Type	Meaning
italic	Terms or phrases that may be found in the Glossary; required function variables that must be entered.
<u>underline</u>	Menu and dialog box options that appear underlined on-screen.
boldface	Information you are asked to type.

Type	Meaning
italic boldface	Optional function variables that can be entered
`special type`	Direct quotations of words that appear on-screen or in a figure.

Elements printed in uppercase include functions, such as SUM(), and cell references, such as A1:G20. File names are also presented in uppercase.

When a direction is given to "click," this means click the left side of the mouse control for those mice with alternate keys. When it is necessary for the right or alternate side of the mouse to be used, the direction "right-click" will be given.

In most cases, keys are represented as they appear on the keyboard. The arrow keys usually are represented by name (for example, the up-arrow key). The Print Screen key is abbreviated PrtSc; Page Up is PgUp; Insert is Ins; and so on. On your keyboard, these key names may be spelled out or abbreviated differently.

When two keys appear together with a plus sign, such as Shift+Ins, press and hold the first key as you press the second key. When two keys appear together without a plus sign, such as End Home, press and release the first key before you press the second key.

 Various toolbar buttons, such as the one next to this paragraph, are used throughout the steps and are identified with a visual icon next to the appropriate step. These icons resemble the on-screen toolbar button and make it easier for you to find them quickly.

Many tasks include warnings, cautions, notes, tips, and troubleshootings. These are described in-depth in this section.

The author has gone to great lengths to protect you from disaster, often warning you of impending, often irreversible danger before you get in over your head. Warnings are just one way this Quick Reference will inform you when you need to know.

> **WARNING** AutoRecover does not save your documents—only certain recovery information! Be sure to save all documents you are working on at frequent intervals.

The completion of some tasks may change several aspects of a document or the way your MS Excel package works in the future. Cautions inform the reader about unforeseen events that may not occur as expected. Cautions are not as severe as warnings, but you will want to read cautionary information.

> **CAUTION** You must save entry and exit macros in the form file. If you save the macros elsewhere and then distribute the form, the entry and exit macros may not run because the macros aren't there.

Notes often advise and direct you while you complete a task. Expect to find pieces of great wisdom while you complete tasks.

NOTE If no misspelled words are found, the Spelling dialog box never appears. Instead, a message box appears and tells you that the spell check is complete.

Tips offer expert input from those who really know the software. Tips often include time-saving solutions and ways to shortcut your way to success. If you're looking for a shortcut key, tips are where you'll find them!

TIP After you define a print area, you can click the Print button on the Standard toolbar to print that worksheet area.

Troubleshootings state problems that you are likely to encounter and how to solve them. These are often the problems that our expert author has most likely encountered or ones that she has experienced causing problems for others. Troubleshootings give the quickest and most appropriate way of addressing the stated problem.

TROUBLESHOOTING **When I select multiple print ranges, each range prints on a separate page. How can I print multiple print ranges on a single page?** You can temporarily hide the rows and columns that separate the ranges and then print them as one print range. Or, you can copy the ranges you want to print to another worksheet, and then print the copied data as a single print range.

All tasks in this book are not for everyone. In some tasks, if you are not already familiar with the instances of use of a task, we will point you to a Special Edition Using book. A Special Edition Using is the most complete core tutorial reference on the topic and can provide you with both background information and tutorial style learning that will help you to understand the topic more thoroughly.

NOTE This feature's task requires understanding of a complex subject. If you are not familiar with this feature, you will probably want to become acquainted with it by reading *Special Edition Using Microsoft Excel 97* for a complete tutorial coverage.

Related Books

No one book can cover all of the needs of every user. Que offers a complete line of Office 97–related titles. Look for Quick References on each of the Office 97 components as well as Windows 95. *Special Edition Using Microsoft Excel 97* is the most complete tutorial and reference volume available for Excel 97, and answers end-user questions with clear, concise, and comprehensive authority. *Special Edition Using Microsoft Office 97 Professional* is the most complete tutorial and reference volume available for Office 97, and Que's *Net Savvy Office 97* concentrates its content on getting the most of Office 97's extensive Internet and intranet features. Ask your bookseller for the availability of other Que titles.

Getting Started

This section of *Microsoft Excel 97 Quick Reference* gets you started with some fundamental tasks that you will use frequently in Excel. You can use the procedures and ideas that you learn here in many of your Excel operations.

You learn how to enter text, numbers, and dates and times. You learn how to use special features that speed data entry, such as AutoComplete and AutoCorrect. In addition, you'll discover how to quickly obtain the Help you need while using Excel. For example, you learn how to use the new Office Assistant to provide detailed assistance as you complete a task.

This section also explains how to name ranges, navigate in the worksheet and in dialog boxes, and select data and other worksheet items. In addition, you learn how to use Undo and Redo, and how to start and exit Excel.

AutoComplete: Entering Duplicate Data

The *AutoComplete* feature makes it easy to enter repeated text items in a column. Instead of typing the same text items over and over, you need to type the entire entry only once in a column. The next time you want to type the same text in the column, you can type the first few letters of this entry. Excel will complete the rest of the entry for you.

For example, you could use this feature in a business expenses worksheet, where you might have categories for Travel, Lodging, Entertainment, and so on. You must type the complete name, such as Travel, the first time you enter these items in a column. The next time, however, you might have to type only the letter **T** to enter the word "Travel."

Steps

1. Type a complete entry into a cell and press Enter.

2. Begin typing the same entry in the next cell down, in the same column; Excel automatically inserts the rest of the entry.

3. Press Enter to accept the entry that Excel suggests, or keep typing if you want to enter a different text item. Press Enter when you finish typing the entry.

You can disable the AutoComplete feature if you find it to be distracting when you enter data. Choose Tools, Options; then click the Edit tab. Clear the Enable AutoComplete for Cell Values check box, and then click OK.

TIP   To see a list of possible cell entries in a column, right-click a cell in that column and choose Pick From List from the shortcut menu. Click an item in the list to insert the entry; or press Esc to clear the list without inserting an item.

NOTE   You can use an apostrophe to reject an AutoCorrect entry that you don't want. For example, if one column entry is "Titles," and you want to enter the letter "T" below it, you can't just type **T** and press Enter as you normally would. First, type the apostrophe, then type **T**, and then press Enter. ■

AutoCorrect: Fixing Typos

AutoCorrect is a feature that automatically corrects common typographical or spelling errors, as you type them. If you accidentally type **teh** in a worksheet, for example, Excel automatically changes the spelling to "the". By default, the AutoCorrect feature already includes many commonly misspelled words; you can, however, enter your own problem words to the AutoCorrect list. You also can add an AutoCorrect entry while in the Spelling dialog box. (See also "Spelling: Running a Spell Check" in the section "Editing Workbooks.")

Steps

1. To create a new AutoCorrect entry, open any workbook and then choose Tools, AutoCorrect.

2. In the Replace text box, enter a common spelling or typographical error. Or, you can also enter an abbreviation for a word or words you often use in your worksheet. Do not enter any spaces in this text box.

3. In the With text box, enter the text as it should appear in the worksheet.

4. Click the Add button to add the new entry to the list; then click OK.

NOTE   Excel AutoCorrects an entry as you type one of the Replace words followed by a space, or when you complete the cell entry. If you want to prevent all automatic corrections, choose Tools, AutoCorrect and clear the Replace Text as You Type check box. ■

Entering: Data in a Selected Range

To speed data entry, you can preselect the range in which you want to enter data. Then, the active cell will move automatically to another cell in the range after you press a specified key. This feature is especially convenient for creating data-entry forms and lists. (See "Entering: Text" or "Entering: Numbers" before you complete this task.)

Steps

1. Select the range in which you want to enter data. The first cell in the selected range is active and appears with a white background.

2. Type the data you want to enter in the first cell.

3. Press Enter to move down one cell, press Shift+Enter to move up one cell, press Tab to move right one cell, or press Shift+Tab to move left one cell.

GETTING STARTED

Entering: Data Series

Excel includes a feature named *AutoFill*, which enables you to enter sequences of values automatically. You start the sequence, and AutoFill analyzes the sequence and continues it for you in a specified range. You can use AutoFill for dates, months, years, positive and negative numbers, and so on. (See "Entering: Numbers" before you complete this task.)

Steps

1. To fill a range with a sequence of numbers, enter the numbers in the first two cells of the range. (These two cells can be in the same column or the same row.)

2. Select the two cells, then position the mouse pointer over the handle in the lower-right corner of the selected range; the pointer changes to a cross.

3. Drag the cross to the end of the range you want to fill with the sequence and release the mouse button; AutoFill completes the sequence of numbers.

 TIP If you want to use dates rather than numbers, enter the first two dates of the sequence in Step 1 above. Excel also recognizes certain text sequences, such as *Qtr 1*, *Qtr 2*, and so on. You can specify your own custom data series as well.

(See also "AutoFill: Entering Custom Data Series" in the section "Data Analysis.")

Entering: Dates and Times

When you type a date or time, Excel converts your entry to a *serial number*. Time is recorded as a decimal fraction of a 24-hour day. If Excel recognizes your entry as a valid date or time format, you see the date or time on-screen. (See also "Formatting: Dates and Times" in the "Formatting" section and "Date and Time Functions" in the "Functions Mini-Reference.")

Steps

1. Select the cell in which you want to enter the date or time.

2. To enter a date or time, enter the date into the cell using any of these formats: 11/6/97, 6-Nov-97, 6-Nov, Nov-97; or, enter the time into the cell using any of these formats: 21:41, 21:41:35, 9:41 PM, 9:41:35 PM.

TIP To quickly enter the current date in a cell, select the cell and press Ctrl+; (semicolon). To enter the current time in a cell, press Ctrl+: (colon). You can combine the date and time in a single cell by separating the date and time with a space.

NOTE You can also enter the dates as **11/6, 11/06/97, Nov-97**, or **November 6, 1997**, but Excel will format the number using one of the formats listed in step 2 above. If Excel does not recognize your entry as a valid date or time format and you type a text date, such as **Nov 6 97**, Excel treats the entry as text and, in an unformatted cell, aligns it to the left. ■

NOTE The first two examples of time formats listed in Step 2 above are from a 24-hour clock. If you use a 12-hour clock, follow the time with a space and either A, AM, P, or PM (in either upper- or lowercase). Be sure that you leave a space before the AM or PM. Do not type a 24-hour clock time with AM or PM. ■

Entering: Numbers

Numbers are constant values containing only the following characters: 0 1 2 3 4 5 6 7 8 9 + - ( ) , / $ % . E e

You can enter integers, such as 24 or 973; decimal fractions, such as 908.37 or 0.72; integer fractions, such as 3 1/4 or 2/3; or scientific notation, such as 5.87137E+3. (See also "Entering: Text" and "Entering: Dates and Times.")

Steps

1. Select the cell in which you want to enter the number.
2. Type the number into the cell. To type a negative number, precede the number with a minus sign (–). Press Enter.

NOTE A cell filled with # signs indicates that the column is not wide enough to display the number correctly. In this case, you need to change the numeric format or widen the column. Drag the right boundary of the column letter to increase the column width. ■

TIP To enter a fraction, type an integer, followed by a space, and then the fraction. If you are entering only the fractional part, type a zero, a space, and then the fraction; otherwise Excel may interpret the entry as a date. Excel reduces fractions when you enter them; if you enter **0 4/8**, for example, Excel converts the entry to 1/2. The formula bar displays the decimal equivalent of the fraction (0.5, in this example).

(See also "Formatting: Numbers" in the section "Formatting.")

Entering: Text

Text entries can include a combination of alphabetical characters, numbers, and symbols. You can type up to 255 characters in a cell. By default, when you enter text in a cell, the text automatically aligns on the left side of the cell.

Occasionally, you may need to enter a number as a text entry. For example, you may need to create a text heading—such as ($000)—that Excel would normally enter as a number. To make Excel accept numbers as text, type an apostrophe (') followed by the number—for example, '39,800. (See also "Entering: Numbers.")

Steps

1. Select the cell in which you want to enter text. Then, type the text into the cell, and press Enter.

2. Text you enter in a cell may appear to be truncated if the cell is not wide enough and if the cell to the right contains data. To automatically fit the column to its widest text entry, double-click the right boundary of the column letter.

(See also "Editing Data: In a Cell" in the section "Editing Workbooks.")

Exiting Excel

Before you exit the Excel program, you should be sure to save all active files (if you want to save recent changes made to them) so you don't lose any data. Excel displays a message box reminding you to save your files if you try to exit the program without saving recent changes. (See "Saving: Workbooks" and "Workbooks: Closing a Workbook" in the section "File Management," before you complete this task.)

Steps

1. Choose <u>F</u>ile, E<u>x</u>it. If you have saved all changes in active workbook files, Excel closes.

2. If a message box appears reminding you to save changes, click <u>Y</u>es to save changes, click <u>N</u>o if you don't want to save changes, or click Cancel to return to Excel.

TIP To quickly exit Excel, click the application Close button (the X at the far right end of the title bar).

Go To: Jumping to a Specific Cell

If you need to jump to another location in the worksheet, and you know the cell address or named range for that location, using the Go To command is usually the quickest way to get there. If you choose a named range with Go To, the entire range is selected.

Steps

1. Display the worksheet containing the cell or named range you want to jump to. Then, choose <u>E</u>dit, <u>G</u>o To; or press F5.

2. In the <u>R</u>eference text box, type the cell address or the named range you want to go to, or select from the list box the named location you want to go to; then click OK.

(See also "Navigating in a Worksheet" and "Selecting: Cells Based on Content.")

Help: Dialog Boxes

Dialog boxes include a question mark in the title bar (beside the Close button), which enables you to obtain Help information on the options and buttons displayed in the dialog box.

Steps

1. To get more information on a button or option in a dialog box, click the Question Mark (?) button in the dialog box title bar. (If the ? button is not visible, press Shift+F1.)

2. Click on the area of the dialog box for which you need Help. A pop-up box appears to explain how to use the button or option.

3. Click the pop-up box to remove it from the screen.

Help: Help Contents and Index

Excel provides an extensive on-line Help system to get you up to speed on workbook tasks. You can access Help at any point to provide assistance, display definitions of common features, and access tips you can use to perform a task more quickly. The Help Contents and Index feature enables you to find detailed Help information on a specific topic.

Steps

1. Choose Help, Contents and Index; then click the Contents tab.

2. Double-click the desired category and click the topic you want; then click Display.

3. View the Help information; then click the Close button when you are done.

TIP   Use the Index tab in the Help Topics dialog box if you want to look up specific words listed in an index format. Click the Index tab, and begin typing the word you are searching for. Then, click the desired index entry in the list box and click Display.

Help: Printing Help Information

You can print most of Excel's on-line Help information for easy reference when you are working with Excel. (See "Help: Help Contents and Index," "Help: Searching for Topics," or "Help: The Office Assistant" before you complete this task.)

Steps

1. Choose Help, Contents and Index; then click either the Contents, Index, or Find tab. Or, click the Office Assistant and type your question.

2. Navigate to the Help window you want to see.

3. In the Help window, click the Options button; then click Print Topic.

4. Make any desired changes in the Print dialog box; then click OK to begin printing.

5. Click the Close button in the Help window when you are done.

Help: Searching for Topics

When you're not sure where to find a Help screen on a certain topic, you can use the Find tab to search for Help using specific keywords, and then choose from a list of selections.

Steps

1. Choose Help, Contents and Index; then click the Find tab.

2. In the text box, type a word that you want to find.

3. In the middle list box, select a word or phrase to narrow your search.

4. In the bottom list box, select the topic you want; then click Display.

5. View the Help information; then click the Close button when you are done.

NOTE   The first time you use Find, Excel builds a word list of Excel terms. This may take a few minutes. ■

GETTING STARTED

Help: The Office Assistant

The *Office Assistant*, a new feature included with Excel and other Microsoft Office applications, provides tips and Help information, and interprets what Help you might need based on your current actions. The Office Assistant is an on-screen, interactive program that can be customized to provide help as you work in Excel.

If you are experienced in Excel and find the Office Assistant to be somewhat bothersome, you can temporarily close the Office Assistant to remove it from the screen. You also can customize options that specify when the Office Assistant should appear.

Steps

1. Click the Office Assistant. (If the Office Assistant doesn't already appear on-screen, click the Office Assistant button in the Standard toolbar; or choose Help, Microsoft Excel Help.)

2. In the text box, type the question or topic for which you want Help; then click the Search button.

3. A Help window or a list of subtopics appears. If you see a subtopics list, click the topic that most closely matches the procedure for which you want Help; then a Help window appears.

4. View the Help information; then click the Close button when you are done.

You may decide that you want to hide the Office Assistant and display it only when you need it. To hide the Office Assistant, click the Close button on the Office Assistant. Click the Office Assistant button in the Standard toolbar to redisplay the Office Assistant. Even if you hide the Office Assistant using this method, however, the Assistant may still display during procedures for which it "guesses" you may need Help. To disable this feature, right-click the Office Assistant and then choose Options. Select the Options tab, clear the Guess Help Topics check box, and then click OK.

To customize how the Office Assistant works, right-click the Office Assistant and choose Options. Select the options you want to use; then click OK.

TIP   When a light bulb appears in the Office Assistant, click it to display a tip related to what you are doing. If the Office Assistant is not visible, click the Office Assistant button in the Standard toolbar, and then click the light bulb to display the tip.

TIP   To change the look of your assistant, insert the Microsoft Excel CD (or the Microsoft Office CD) in your CD drive, then right-click the Office Assistant and select Choose Assistant. In the Gallery tab, use the Next and Back buttons to scroll through the different assistants. When you see the assistant you want to use, click OK.

Help: Tip of the Day

The Tip of the Day feature provides an easy way to familiarize yourself with some of Excel's capabilities. When this feature is enabled, a tip on using Excel appears each time you start Excel. You can also see additional tips while you are using Excel. (See also "Help: The Office Assistant.")

Steps

1. Click the Office Assistant. (If the Office Assistant doesn't already appear on-screen, click the Office Assistant button in the Standard toolbar.). Click Options.

2. In the Options tab, click the Show the Tip of the Day at Startup check box; then click OK.

3. To see additional tips while you are using Excel, you can access the Office Assistant and click the Tips option.

TIP   If you see a light bulb displayed next to the Office Assistant, click it to see a helpful tip on your current actions.

Help: Toolbar Buttons

Excel provides ScreenTips to help you remember the names and functions of the toolbar buttons. *ScreenTips* are the small pop-up labels that appear next to a toolbar button when you move the mouse pointer onto the button and pause. If you need more detailed information on using a toolbar button than the brief description that is displayed in a ScreenTip, you can use the What's This? Help feature.

Steps

1. To get more information on a toolbar button (in addition to the ScreenTip), choose Help, What's This?; or press Shift+F1.

2. Click on the toolbar button for which you need Help. A pop-up box appears to explain how to use the button.

3. Click the pop-up box to remove it from the screen.

 TIP To turn ScreenTips on or off, choose View, Toolbars, Customize; then click the Options tab and select (or clear) the Show ScreenTips on Toolbars check box. Click Close.

Microsoft IntelliMouse: Navigating

The IntelliMouse makes navigating in Excel 97 easier. The Microsoft IntelliMouse pointing device includes a small wheel between the left and right mouse buttons. The wheel rolls forward and backward, and depresses. The wheel button on the IntelliMouse will function only if you install IntelliPoint 2.0 (or later) software and you are using applications that take advantage of the IntelliMouse.

Steps

■ To scroll the worksheet a few rows at a time using the IntelliMouse, roll the wheel forward to scroll up and backward to scroll down.

■ To pan in the worksheet using the IntelliMouse, hold down the wheel as you drag in any direction to quickly move the window in that direction.

■ To expand or collapse worksheet outlines using the IntelliMouse, hold down the Shift key as you roll the wheel.

(See also "Microsoft IntelliMouse: Zooming.")

Microsoft IntelliMouse: Zooming

The Microsoft IntelliMouse pointing device includes a small wheel between the left and right mouse buttons. The wheel rolls forward and backward and depresses. The IntelliMouse makes zooming in Excel 97 easier.

NOTE The wheel button on the IntelliMouse will function only if you install IntelliPoint 2.0 (or later) software and you are using applications that take advantage of the IntelliMouse. ■

Steps

1. To zoom in a worksheet using the IntelliMouse, first hold down the Ctrl key.

2. Roll the wheel to zoom to a different magnification—between 10% and 100%.

TIP If you use the IntelliMouse to zoom more often than you use it to scroll in a worksheet, you can set the wheel button so that it automatically zooms instead of scrolls. Choose Tools, Options, click the General tab, and then select Zoom on Roll with IntelliMouse. Click OK.

(See also "Microsoft IntelliMouse: Navigating" in this section and "Zooming: The Worksheet Display" in the "Customizing" section.)

Naming Cells and Ranges

Excel enables you to assign a name to a cell or range because names are usually easier to remember than cell references. It's much easier to recall a name like Qtr1, for example, than the cell address that refers to that range, such as D4:D6. Also, the meaning of the formula =Sales-Expenses is much clearer than the formula =C12-C25. Another advantage to using names is that names automatically adjust when you insert or delete rows or columns—you don't need to redefine the name.

Steps

1. To define a name, select the cell or range you want to name and click the arrow beside the name box in the formula bar.

2. Type the name for the selected cell or range; then press Enter.

NOTE If you enter a name that is already in use, the cell or range with that name is selected; the original selection is not assigned the name. To redefine or delete an existing name, you must use the Insert, Name, Define command. ▓

CAUTION When you create or define names, they do not automatically appear in existing formulas in the worksheet. If you create the names after you create the formulas, you need to apply the names to the formulas by using the Insert, Name, Apply command.

Navigating in a Worksheet

To enter data in a cell, select ranges, and view areas of the worksheet, you first must move the cell pointer to the cell you want to manipulate. The active cell in the worksheet is indicated by a highlighted border. In Excel, you can move the cell pointer with both the mouse and keyboard.

Keys Useful for Worksheet Navigation

Although the mouse has become the tool of choice for many and is required for some tasks, there are still times when keyboard navigation can be quite useful. The following table summarizes the keys or key combinations you can use to navigate the Excel worksheet.

Worksheet Navigation Keys

Key	Action
↓ or Enter	Moves down one row
↑ or Shift+Enter	Moves up one row
→ or Tab	Moves right one column
← or Shift+Tab	Moves left one column
Page Down	Moves down one screen
Page Up	Moves up one screen
Alt+Page Down	Moves right one screen
Alt+Page Up	Moves left one screen
Home	Moves to the first cell in the current row
Ctrl+Home	Moves to cell A1 of the current worksheet
End, Home	Moves to the bottom right corner of the current worksheet
Ctrl+Page Down	Moves to the next sheet in the workbook
Ctrl+Page Up	Moves to the previous sheet in the workbook

Steps

- To move the cell pointer with the mouse, click the cell you want to make active; if that cell is not visible, use the scroll bars to move to the area of the worksheet you want, and then click the cell.

- To move the cell pointer with the keyboard, use any keys or key combinations described in the table above.

(See also "Go To: Jumping to a Specific Cell.")

Selecting: Cells and Ranges

In many Excel commands, such as to copy a range of cells or apply a cell format, you first must select the range of cells you want the command to affect. You can select cells with the mouse or keyboard. (If you want to navigate the worksheet

GETTING STARTED

using the keyboard, see "Navigating in a Worksheet" before completing this task.)

Steps

- ■ To select a single cell, click that cell or use the keyboard navigation keys to move to that cell.

- ■ To select a range of cells, click the first cell in the range; then hold down the mouse button and drag to the opposite corner of the range. Release the mouse button.

- ■ If you want to select a large range that is not entirely visible on-screen, select the first cell in the range. Then scroll the worksheet until you see the opposite corner. Hold down the Shift key, and then click the opposite corner of the range. All cells between the two corners are selected.

Selecting: Cells Based on Content

In addition to using Go To to jump to a particular cell or named range, you also can use Go To to select cells by content or relationship to formulas. This command is useful if you want to select only cells containing items such as comments, constants, formulas, conditional formats, or objects like charts. (See also "Go To: Jumping to a Specific Cell.")

Steps

1. To check the entire worksheet for a specific cell content, select a single cell; to check only cells within a range, select a range of cells.

2. Choose Edit, Go To; or press F5.

3. From the Go To dialog box, choose Special and select the desired option; then click OK.

 TIP　After you select cells with Edit, Go To, Special, you can retain the selections and move between the cells by pressing Tab, Shift+Tab, Enter, or Shift+Enter.

Selecting: Multiple Ranges

While working in Excel, you may want to preselect more than one range of data. This saves time when formatting multiple ranges of data with the same formatting, such as the currency number format. Instead of selecting ranges individually and formatting them, you can format all ranges at once. (See "Selecting: Cells and Ranges" before you complete this task.)

Steps

1. Select the first range of cells.

2. Hold down the Ctrl key; then click and drag to select the next range of cells.

3. Repeat Step 2 until you have selected all the ranges you want.

Selecting: Rows and Columns

You can perform some tasks more quickly if you select an entire row or column at one time. You also can select multiple adjacent or nonadjacent rows or columns. If you want to increase the column width of multiple adjacent columns while keeping them the same width, for example, preselect those columns and then size them as needed.

Steps

■ To select a single column, click the column heading. To select multiple adjacent columns, drag the pointer across the column headings. To select multiple nonadjacent columns, press Ctrl and click each column heading.

■ To select a single row, click the row heading. To select multiple adjacent rows, drag the pointer across the row headings. To select multiple nonadjacent rows, press Ctrl and click each row heading.

 TIP You also can use the keyboard to select the current row or column. To select the current row, press Shift+space bar. To select the current column, press Ctrl+space bar.

Selecting: Worksheets

You can use the sheet tabs at the bottom of the worksheet area to select the desired worksheet in the current workbook. You also can select multiple worksheets if you want to group the worksheets and perform actions on all selected worksheets. (See "Grouping Worksheets" in the section "Editing Workbooks.")

Steps

■ To select a worksheet in the current workbook, click the sheet tab. The worksheet displays.

■ If you want to select all cells in the current worksheet, click the gray rectangle that appears at the intersection of the row headers and column headers.

CAUTION   When the entire worksheet is selected, any command or action you perform will affect the entire worksheet. If you press the Delete key while the worksheet is selected, for example, you will delete all the data in the worksheet.

Starting Excel

To start the Excel program, you first must start Windows 95. If you have not yet installed Excel, follow the installation instructions provided with the program.

Steps

1. To start Excel, click the Start button in the Windows taskbar.

2. Choose Programs, Microsoft Excel.

(See also "Exiting Excel" in this section, and "Startup: Controlling Excel's Startup" and "Startup: Setting Startup Switches" in the "Customizing" section.)

Undo and Redo

Excel provides a built-in safety net, the Undo command, that enables you to reverse your most recent action and return your workbook to its previous state. You must use Undo immediately after the most recent action you want to undo. The Undo command (in the Edit menu) changes to show the most recent action performed; if the Undo command is dimmed, you cannot undo the most recent action. Not all commands can be undone—you cannot undo a save operation, for example.

If you want to reverse the action of the most recent Undo command, use the Redo command. You can select the Undo or Redo commands multiple times to step back through your most recent actions or to redo the last set of actions that have been undone. However, you cannot undo a previous action without also undoing all actions that you performed after it; that is why you should choose Undo immediately following the command or action you want to reverse.

Steps

   ■ To undo your most recent entry or command, choose Edit, Undo; or click the Undo button in the Standard toolbar.

   ■ If you want to redo the entry or command you just undid, choose Edit, Redo; or click the Redo button in the Standard toolbar. Note that the Redo command is unavailable until you choose Undo.

■ If you want to undo or repeat multiple actions (not just the most recent action), click the arrow beside either the Undo or Redo button on the Standard toolbar. A drop-down list of the previous actions that can be undone or redone appears. Select the actions you want to undo or redo.

NOTE   The command name in the Edit menu changes to Can't Undo if you cannot undo the most recent action. ■

Charts and Graphics

Charts enable you to present worksheet data in graphical form. When you create a chart, the worksheet data used to create the chart is linked to it. When the worksheet data changes, the chart is updated to reflect those changes. Excel provides many features for creating and formatting charts. The Chart Wizard leads you step-by-step through the process. You can change chart types, add elements to a chart (such as titles or legends), and format chart elements (such as numbers, fonts, and styles).

Excel also enables you to add graphic elements to your worksheet. You can import graphics from other programs, insert *clip art* objects, or use the Drawing toolbar to create objects such as arrows, rectangles, and WordArt. After you draw an object in the worksheet, you can edit, rotate, flip, copy or move, size, or add shadows or 3-D effects to the object.

You can use the data map feature to present geographical data from your worksheets in map form. *Data mapping* enables you to see the relationships between numbers and geographic features.

Adding: Chart Arrows

You can use arrows to identify chart elements that you want people to notice, such as sales data that is higher or lower than expected, or a specific trend that may be occurring in the chart data. Frequently, you may use a text label to include explanatory text, and you can draw the arrow from the label to the chart element. (See also "Adding: Chart Data Labels.")

Steps

1. Select the chart, and then display the Drawing toolbar by clicking the Drawing button on the Standard toolbar.

2. Click the Arrow button on the Drawing toolbar. The pointer changes to a crosshair.

3. Click in the chart where you want the tail of the arrow to appear, hold down the mouse button while you drag across the chart to where you want the head of the arrow, and then release the mouse button.

Move an existing arrow by selecting it and then dragging it to the location you want. To change the length or position of the arrow, select the arrow and then drag the white square at either end of the arrow. To delete an arrow, select the arrow and then press Delete.

TIP You can format the arrow by adding color, changing the thickness of the line, or selecting a different shape for the arrowhead. Double-click the arrow, then make the selections you want in the Format Autoshape dialog box.

(See also "Drawing an Object" and "AutoShapes.")

Adding: Chart Data Labels

You can attach labels to data points on your chart, which helps the viewer interpret the data in a chart more easily. *Data labels* can represent the value for that data point or the category axis label associated with the data point. You can attach data labels to individual data points, a single data series, or all data points in a chart.

Steps

1. Within the chart, select the data point(s) to which you want to add labels: to select an entire data series, click any point in the series; to select an individual point in the series, click the data point twice; to insert labels on all data points for all series, click outside the chart to select the entire chart.

2. Choose Chart, Chart Options; then click the Data Labels tab in the Chart Options dialog box.

3. Select the Data Labels option you want to use, such as Show Value, Show Percent, or Show Label. (Depending on the chart type, some options may not be available.) Click OK.

To remove existing data labels from a chart, display the Data Labels tab of the Chart Options dialog box. Then select the None option and click OK.

NOTE Numeric data labels display with the format of the corresponding cell(s) in the worksheet. To change a number's format in the chart, you can format its worksheet cell. If you want to format the data values directly in the chart, select the labels and choose Format, Selected Labels; then click the Number tab and change to the format you want. ▪

TIP You can add floating text in a chart to label an arrow or other chart elements. Select any nontext object in the chart, type the text, and press Enter. To move the text label, press and hold down Ctrl, then drag the label to the position you want. (See also "Adding: Chart Arrows.")

(See also "Formatting: Chart Data Series.")

Adding: Chart Gridlines

Use gridlines to help viewers compare markers and read values in a chart. If you use the Chart Wizard to create a chart, Excel enables you to add gridlines as you are creating the chart.

You can add gridlines that originate from either the category or value axis, or both. In a 3-D chart, you can also add gridlines for the Z axis (chart depth). You can choose whether to display gridlines for major divisions on an axis or minor divisions (including points between major divisions).

Steps

1. After selecting the chart, choose Chart, Chart Options; then click the Gridlines tab in the Chart Options dialog box.

2. Select the type of gridlines you want to add; then click OK.

To remove gridlines from a chart, display the Gridlines tab of the Chart Options dialog box, and then clear the boxes for the gridlines you want to remove.

TIP Avoid using too many gridlines in a chart because they may make the chart confusing and difficult to read.

Adding: Chart Legends

A *legend* explains the markers or symbols used in a chart. If you use the Chart Wizard to create a chart, Excel creates a legend by default, based on labels from the shorter side of the worksheet data series. If your chart does not include a legend, you can easily add one. You also can format a legend with border, pattern, and font selections.

Steps

1. Select the chart.

2. Choose Chart, Chart Options; then click the Legend tab in the Chart Options dialog box.

3. Choose Show Legend. Then select the Placement you want for the legend: Bottom, Corner, Top, Right, or Left. Click OK.

You can move the legend by selecting it and then dragging the legend to the location you want. To resize the legend, select it and then drag one of the black handles surrounding the legend. To delete a legend, select it and press Delete.

TIP To format the legend, right-click the legend and choose Format Legend from the shortcut menu. Make the selections you want from the Format Legend dialog box and then click OK.

Adding: Chart Titles

You can add titles to help explain the data in your chart. Normally, you include a main chart title as well as titles for the category and value axes. If you use the Chart Wizard to create a chart, Excel enables you to add chart titles as you are creating the chart. You also can choose to add chart titles later or modify existing chart titles.

Steps

1. After selecting the chart, choose Chart, Chart Options; then click the Titles tab in the Chart Options dialog box.

2. Select the text box for the title you want to add (such as Chart Title) and type the title; then click OK.

You can move the title by selecting it and then dragging an edge of the title to the location you want. To delete a title, select it and press Delete.

TIP   To format a chart title, right-click the title and choose Format Title from the shortcut menu. Make the selections you want from the Format Title dialog box and then click OK.

(See also "Formatting: Chart Titles and Labels.")

Adding: Chart Trendlines

You can add a trendline to a chart to show the direction of the charted data and to make predictions. Regression analysis, a technique that describes relationships among variables, is used to create the trendline from the chart data. You can choose from among five types of regression lines or calculate a line that displays moving averages.

Steps

1. After selecting the chart, choose Chart, Add Trendline; then select the Type tab in the Add Trendline dialog box.

2. Select the data series for which you want to create a trendline in the Based On Series list.

3. Select from among the six Trend/Regression types: Linear, Logarithmic, Polynomial, Power, Exponential, and Moving Average. For more detailed information on these types, click the question mark in the title bar of the dialog box, and then click the option for which you want more information.

4. Select the Options tab if you want to set any additional options for the trendline, such as the Trendline Name or Forecast options. Click OK.

Adding: Graphic Backgrounds

You can add a graphic background, similar to a watermark, to your worksheets. This feature can dramatically improve the appearance of forms and reports. A background also is a unique way of inserting a company logo in a worksheet without using a prominent graphic.

When Excel adds a graphic background, the graphic is tiled, or repeated across the full width and height of the worksheet. Tiling requires no additional memory for multiple graphics than it does for a single graphic. Excel provides some samples of graphic backgrounds, such as a brick wall or a deco design. You also can use pictures of your own as well as Web page backgrounds.

Steps

1. Open the worksheet in which you want to add a graphic background; then choose Format, Sheet, Background. The Sheet Background dialog box appears.

2. Select the graphic file you want to use. Check the \MSOffice\Clipart folder for samples provided with Excel. Then click Open.

To delete a graphic background, choose Format, Sheet, Delete Background.

TIP   Most graphic backgrounds look better if you remove gridlines from the display. Choose Tools, Options; then click the View tab. Clear the Gridlines check box and then click OK.

Adding: New Chart Data

You can add new data to existing charts, whether you created the chart automatically or manually. You can add a new data series to a chart, add new data points to existing data series, or change the entire range of data the chart uses.

If you are working in a separate chart sheet or an embedded chart that has been selected in a worksheet, you can use the Chart, Add Data command. You can use the Chart, Source Data command to edit existing data series or add new series. (See "Creating: Chart Wizard Charts" before you complete this task.)

Steps

1. To add new data to an embedded chart in a worksheet, select the data you want to add from that worksheet.

2. Point to an edge of the selected range until the pointer changes to an arrow. Drag the data anywhere onto the chart and release the mouse button.

NOTE If the chart to which you want to add new data resides on a separate chart sheet (instead of being embedded within a worksheet), the procedure is a bit different. Select the chart sheet; then choose Chart, Add Data. Enter the Range for the new data and click OK. The data is added to the chart. ■

AutoShapes

AutoShapes are ready-made shapes provided with Excel that you can add to worksheets, chart sheets, or embedded charts in a worksheet. These shapes are arranged in groups such as flowchart symbols, stars and banners, block arrows, and connectors. (See also "Drawing an Object.")

You can use AutoShapes to create an entire flowchart in a worksheet by adding flowchart symbols and using connector symbols or block arrows to connect the flowchart symbols. You can easily add text to most AutoShapes by selecting the shape and typing the text you want to insert.

CHARTS AND GRAPHICS

Steps

1. Select the worksheet, chart sheet, or embedded chart in a worksheet to which you want to add an AutoShape. Then click the Drawing button on the Standard toolbar to display the Drawing toolbar.

2. Click the AutoShapes button on the Drawing toolbar. A pop-up menu appears.

3. Point to a category of AutoShapes, such as Stars and Banners, and then click the shape you want to use.

4. Click on the area within the worksheet, chart sheet, or embedded chart where you want the AutoShape to appear.

You can move the AutoShape by selecting it and then dragging the shape to the location you want. To resize the shape, select it and then drag one of the handles surrounding the shape. To maintain the original proportions of the shape, hold down the Shift key and then drag one of the corner handles. To delete an AutoShape, select it and press Delete.

TIP   To format the AutoShape by adding colors, changing borders, or adding shadow or 3-D effects, select the shape and use the tools on the Drawing toolbar. For additional formatting options, right-click the AutoShape and choose Format AutoShape from the shortcut menu. Make the selections you want and then click OK.

Changing Chart Types

You can change an Excel chart type to represent another type of data. You can change to any of the chart types that Excel offers—bar charts, line charts, pie charts, or special custom charts like floating bar charts.

When to Change Chart Types

You should use an appropriate chart type for the data you want to chart. The following list illustrates some common Excel chart types and explains their purpose. For more detailed information on all the chart types and examples of their use, search on "chart types, example" in Excel help.

- **Column chart.** Illustrates individual values at a specific point in time and is suitable for almost any data type, particularly side-by-side comparisons of numerous data values.

- **Bar chart.** Same as a column chart, but displays bars horizontally rather than vertically.

- **Line chart.** Illustrates linear or unbroken changes in a large number of values.

- **Pie chart.** Shows the relationship of parts to the whole and to each other, so that the reader can assess and compare items readily.

- **XY (scatter) chart.** Plots two groups of numbers as one series of XY coordinates. Useful as a diagnostic tool when looking for heavy occurrences or absences of data. Commonly used in scientific applications.

- **Area chart.** Shows how volume changes over time and emphasizes the amount of change. Useful for giving a bigger sense of "mass" of a change or concept.

Steps

1. Right-click in a blank area of the chart and choose Chart Type from the shortcut menu.

2. In the Chart Type dialog box, click the Standard Types or Custom Types tab.

3. Select the chart type you want and then click OK. Resize the chart by dragging one of the chart handles, if necessary.

NOTE In some cases, data may be more effective when presented in a table or text chart. Don't overload your charts with too many data points. Combine data into logical units such as first quarter, second quarter, and so on to make your charts more effective. ■

Clip Art

Clip art is a collection of graphics and pictures that is available for use in programs such as Excel. Clip art enables you to illustrate ideas with pictures. You can use clip art in place of columns or bars in a chart to add interest to a presentation, for example. You also can use clip art to create a company logo for a company invoice or expense statement. Many of Excel's built-in templates include a placeholder for you to insert a clip art logo. Be careful not to overdo your use of clip art; generally one effective use of clip art in a worksheet is sufficient. (See also "Creating: Picture Charts" and "Template Wizard: Using Excel's Templates" in the section "Data Analysis.")

Where to Find Clip Art

Many clip art collections are sold in categories like business graphics, medical graphics, entertainment graphics, and so on. To locate clip art, look for ads in the back of computer magazines, particularly desktop publishing magazines. You also may find clip art packages available for purchase at your local software store.

Some programs, such as Excel, include free clip art collections. You use the Microsoft Clip Gallery in Excel to easily access these clip art images. You also can find collections of clip art on the Internet and online services such as CompuServe, America Online, and Prodigy. (See also "Importing Graphics.")

Steps

1. In your worksheet, select the cell where you want the upper-left corner of the clip art to appear.

2. Choose Insert, Picture, Clip Art. Select the Clip Art tab in the Microsoft Clip Gallery dialog box.

3. Select a category from the list box on the left side of the dialog box. Then click the clip art symbol you want to use and choose Insert.

NOTE If you cannot access the Microsoft Clip Gallery, you probably did not install this feature with Excel. For more information on how to install the Clip Gallery, search on "clip art" in Excel help. Then choose "Insert an imported picture or clip art" and follow the instructions. ▪

Creating: Automatic Charts

If you want to create a chart using the default chart type (normally a column chart) and place this chart on a separate chart sheet in the workbook, you can use the shortcut procedure listed below to quickly create the chart. Otherwise, if you want to use a different chart type or embed the chart in the worksheet that contains the source data, use the Chart Wizard to create the chart. (See also "Creating: Chart Wizard Charts.")

Steps

1. Select the worksheet data you want to chart.
2. Press the F11 key. The chart appears automatically in a separate chart sheet.2

Creating: Chart Wizard Charts

In Excel, you most often create charts using the *Chart Wizard*. Although the Chart Wizard steps you through the entire process of creating a chart, you can create the chart more quickly by accepting some or all of the defaults that Excel suggests. You can add a chart directly to the worksheet or you can create a separate chart sheet in the workbook. (See also "Creating: Automatic Charts.")

Steps

1. Select the worksheet data you want to chart and then click the Chart Wizard button on the Standard toolbar.
2. Select the type of chart you want in the Chart Type list; then choose Next.

3. Verify the chart data range and specify whether you want to plot the series in Rows or Columns; then choose Next.

4. Click the appropriate tab and select the chart options you want, such as titles and data labels; then choose Next.

5. Select whether you want the chart to appear as a new sheet in the workbook or as a chart object (an embedded chart) in an existing worksheet. Choose Finish.

TIP To move a chart, select it and drag an edge of the chart to the location you want. To change the size or proportions of the chart, drag one of the black handles along the borders until the chart is sized and proportioned the way you want.

Creating: Picture Charts

Excel charts can use pictures as markers in place of columns, bars, lines, or as backgrounds. You can use this feature to make picture charts that draw attention and then communicate the information. When showing dollar amounts, for example, you can use money bags of varying sizes for each marker.

Steps

1. In the chart, right-click the data series that you want to replace with a picture, and choose Format Data Series. You can also select the plot or chart area if you want the picture to fill the background area of the chart.

2. In the Format Data Series dialog box, click the Patterns tab; then choose Fill Effects and click the Picture tab.

3. Choose Select Picture. In the Look In box, change to the drive and folder where the image is stored. Select the file for the picture you want to insert; then click OK.

4. Choose other options on the Picture tab if you want. Experiment with various options (Stretch, Stack, or Stack and Scale) to see which effect looks best on your chart. For 3-D charts, select the options you want from the Apply To group. Click OK twice to return to the worksheet.

(See "Clip Art" for sources of picture collections.)

Drawing an Object

Excel enables you to add graphics to your worksheets by drawing objects inside the worksheet itself. The drawing buttons on the Drawing toolbar enable you to create ovals, rectangles, polygons, arrows, and even freehand objects. Excel 97 includes additional drawing tools as well as new tools to assist you with manipulating drawn objects.

By combining drawn objects, you can create all kinds of images. Drawn objects can enhance your worksheet reports, add annotation elements to your charts, and generally spruce up your worksheets.

You can use the AutoShapes tool on the Drawing toolbar to quickly draw more complex shapes such as stars and flowchart symbols. (See also "AutoShapes.")

Steps

1. To display the Drawing toolbar, click the Drawing button on the Standard toolbar; or choose <u>V</u>iew, <u>T</u>oolbars, Drawing.

2. From the Drawing toolbar, select a shape button such as the Arrow, Rectangle, or Oval. If you need more than one copy of a particular shape, double-click the selected button. That button stays selected until you click the same button or click another tool.

3. Click and drag in the worksheet to draw the object, then release the mouse button. If you just click in the worksheet, the object appears with the default dimensions.

4. Change the selected object's location by dragging the object; change the selected object's size by dragging the sizing handles.

5. Use the Drawing toolbar buttons such as Fill Color, Line Color, and Line Style to format the object's appearance.

To delete an object, select it and then press Delete.

CHARTS AND GRAPHICS

TIP To create a perfect square or circle, hold down the Shift key while drawing a rectangle or oval. To add a shadow or 3-D appearance to the object, select the object and then click the Shadow or 3-D button on the Drawing toolbar. Choose the effect you want from the palette.

Drawn Objects: Copying and Moving

Excel enables you to easily create exact duplicates of existing objects in your worksheet. You also can move objects to a different position in the worksheet.

Steps

1. To copy an object, press and hold down the Ctrl key. Then click and drag the object you want to copy. As you drag, a copy of the object moves with the pointer. Release the mouse button.

2. To move an object, select the object and then drag it to the position you want.

Drawn Objects: Freehand Drawings

Although you can use ready-made AutoShapes to save time when drawing objects, you sometimes may need to manually create an unusually shaped object. The Lines option on the AutoShapes button enables you to create these freehand drawings: curves, freeform polygons, and scribbles. (See "Drawing an Object" and "AutoShapes" before you complete this task.)

Steps

1. Click the AutoShapes button in the Drawing toolbar and then choose Lines.

2. Choose the freehand object you want to draw: Curve, Freeform, or Scribble.

3. To create a curve or freeform object, click in the worksheet to begin the object, then move to a new point and click where you want the line to end. A curve or line

appears between those two points. Click as many points as you want the object to include. When you are finished, double-click the last point.

To create a scribble, hold down the mouse button the entire time you are drawing your object in the worksheet. Release the mouse button when you are finished.

4. To create a closed drawing, right-click the freehand drawing, and choose Close Curve from the shortcut menu.

Drawn Objects: Grouping

When drawing objects, you may find that you want to format or edit many existing objects at once. Instead of having to select each object and format it individually, you can group the objects so they all act as if they are part of the same object. When you group objects, their individual handles disappear and the entire group is surrounded by sizing handles.

Steps

1. Click the first object in the group to select it.

2. Hold down the Shift key and click all other objects that you want in the group. All the objects should remain selected.

Draw ▾

3. Choose the Draw button on the Drawing toolbar and choose Group from the pop-up menu. You can now move or format the objects as a group.

To ungroup a set of grouped objects, select the group. Then choose the Draw button on the Drawing toolbar and choose Ungroup from the pop-up menu.

Drawn Objects: Rearranging

As you create a drawing, you sometimes add objects on top of one another in stacked layers. If you need to adjust the order of these objects, you can use the Order options available from the Draw button on the Drawing toolbar. You may choose to move the bottom object to the top, for example, to adjust its order in the stack. To get the arrangement you want, you may need to rearrange several objects in a specific order.

Steps

1. Select the object that you want to move behind or in front of other objects.

 2. Choose the Draw button on the Drawing toolbar and then choose Order.

3. Choose the option you want. The Bring to Front and Send to Back options move the object all the way to the front or back of the selected objects in one step. The Bring Forward and Send Backward options move the object forward or backward one object at a time.

Drawn Objects: Rotating and Flipping

You can adjust the placement and position of a drawn object by using the Rotate or Flip option on the Draw button of the Drawing toolbar. You can rotate the object left or right, 90 degrees at a time. You can also flip the object horizontally or vertically to reverse the position of the object. This feature is useful when you want a mirror image of an object.

Steps

1. Select the object you want to rotate or flip.

 2. Choose the Draw button on the Drawing toolbar and then choose Rotate or Flip.

3. Choose an option from the Rotate or Flip menu, such as Rotate Left, Rotate Right, Flip Horizontally, or Flip Vertically.

 TIP Click the Free Rotate button on the Drawing toolbar if you need more flexibility when rotating or flipping objects. Drag one of the rotation handles surrounding the object to the position you want. Click the Free Rotate button again to disable the feature.

Drawn Objects: Sizing

After you've drawn an object in the worksheet, you may decide to enlarge or reduce the size of an object. You also may want to change the proportions of the object.

Steps

1. After selecting the object, click and drag one of the object's handles in the direction you want to resize. Drag a side handle to resize the object horizontally or vertically. Drag a corner handle to resize both sides simultaneously.

2. Release the mouse button to end resizing.

TIP   Hold down the Shift key while dragging a corner handle to maintain the proportions of the object.

Formatting: Chart Axes

When you create a chart, Excel uses the default settings for the axis style, tick marks, and scaling. Tick marks are the small lines that appear on an axis, similar to measurement lines on a ruler. You can customize the axis, changing the style of the line used for the axis, the tick marks, the positioning of the tick-mark labels, and the scaling of the axis.

Steps

1. Right-click the axis line you want to customize and choose Format Axis from the shortcut menu.

2. In the Format Axis dialog box, click the Patterns tab and then select one of the Axis options.

3. Select the options you want from the Major Tick Mark Type and Minor Tick Mark Type areas.

4. Select an option in the Tick Mark Labels area to specify where to position the tick-mark labels.

5. Check to see if the axis line in the Sample box looks the way you want, and make additional changes on the Patterns tab if necessary; then click OK.

CHARTS AND GRAPHICS

Formatting: Chart Data Series

You can enhance the presentation of your data by adding error bars or data labels to a data series. Use error bars to visually display the margin of error in a data series. Data labels are typically used to explain the data points in a chart. You also can change the gap width between the columns in a column chart and make other formatting changes.

Steps

1. In the worksheet, right-click the data series you want to format and choose Format Data Series from the shortcut menu.

2. In the Format Data Series dialog box, click the tab containing the options you want to change (such as Error Bars, Data Labels, Series Order, or Options).

3. Modify the options as you want; then click OK.

Formatting: Chart Fonts and Styles

You can change fonts and styles in charts just as you change them in worksheets. First, select the elements you want to change, and then make the changes.

Steps

1. Click the text element you want to format. If you want to format only individual characters within a text element, select those characters.

2. Click a button on the Formatting toolbar for the format you want to change. For example, click the Font Size button to change the point size of the font, or click the Italic button to italicize the text.

TIP   To see additional font options that don't appear on the toolbar, right-click the text element you want to format. Choose Format from the shortcut menu and make your selections from the Font tab; then click OK.

Formatting: Chart Numbers

You can format the numbers in a chart just as you format the numbers in a worksheet. For example, you can add dollar signs to the numbers on the value (Y) axis or change the format of numbers used as data labels.

If the numbers in the worksheet you used to create the chart are formatted, the numbers used in the value axis in the chart are formatted the same way. You can override this formatting, however, or add formatting if the numbers in the chart are unformatted.

Steps

1. Right-click the object whose numbers you want to format and then choose Format from the shortcut menu.

2. In the Format dialog box, click the Number tab and then select the number format you want from the Category list.

3. The Format dialog box changes to display options that relate to your category choice. Change any options you want; then click OK.

 TIP To return the formatting to the number formats that appear in the source worksheet, select the Linked to Source option in the Format dialog box.

Formatting: Chart Objects

Excel provides many options and commands that enable you to enhance your chart objects. Chart objects include titles, legends, axes, data series, and so on. You can easily add or change the colors, patterns, and borders of objects in a chart. Excel 97 includes several new patterns, including interesting gradients and textures, that you can use in your charts.

Steps

1. Right-click the chart object and choose Format from the shortcut menu.

CHARTS AND GRAPHICS

2. In the Format dialog box, click the Patterns tab.

3. In the Border group, select the border options you want. In the Area group, select the color you want.

4. To select a fill effect (pattern), choose Fill Effects. Click one of the tabs and choose the pattern you want; then click OK twice to return to the worksheet.

 TIP If you want to change the color or pattern for the chart background, right-click any edge of the chart and choose Format Chart Area from the shortcut menu. Make your selections and then click OK.

Formatting: Chart Titles and Labels

For some text objects in charts, such as titles, you can change both the horizontal and vertical *alignment,* as well as the *orientation* (or rotation) of the text. For other objects, such as the labels on the axes, you can change only the orientation. You can rotate axis titles or text boxes that contain explanations.

Steps

1. Right-click the text object and choose Format from the shortcut menu.

2. In the Format dialog box, click the Alignment tab; then select the alignment options you want from the Horizontal and Vertical drop-down lists.

3. Drag the pointer in the Orientation box up or down to change the orientation of the text, or specify a value in the Degrees spin box between 90 and –90 degrees; then click OK.

 TIP To quickly select a stacked orientation, reading top to bottom, click the box to the left of the Orientation gauge.

Importing Graphics

The procedure for importing graphics (or pictures) into your worksheets is similar to the way you insert clip art images. You can insert a picture into your worksheet without opening the program you used to create the picture. After you import a graphic, you can move, resize, or format the graphic. (See also "Clip Art.")

Steps

1. Select the cell in the worksheet where you want the upper-left corner of the graphic to appear. (Because the picture is inserted as an object, you can later move it to a different location.)

2. Choose Insert, Picture, From File. The Insert Picture dialog box appears.

3. Locate the graphic file you want to import; then choose Insert.

4. The graphic appears in the worksheet, and the Picture toolbar appears. Use the buttons on the Picture toolbar to modify or format the graphic if you want.

Maps: Adding New Map Data

You can add new data to an existing data map at any time. You can insert data in existing categories or add entirely new categories (columnar data) to display in the map. (See "Maps: Creating a Basic Data Map" before you complete this task.)

Steps

1. In the worksheet, type the new data in its own column (adjacent to the existing columns of data).

2. Double-click the map to activate it; then choose Insert, Data.

3. When the Microsoft Map dialog box appears, drag across the entire data range you want to map (existing data and new data); then click OK.

CHARTS AND GRAPHICS

4. The Microsoft Map Control now includes additional buttons that correspond to the data you have added. Drag the new column buttons into the working area to add the data to the map.

 5. If necessary, click the Map Refresh button on the Map toolbar to update the map.

NOTE   If you want only to insert data in existing categories, select cells in the middle of the current data range; then, from the Insert menu, choose Cells. Select the Shift Cells Down option and click OK. Enter the new region name and data where you inserted the cells and then click the Map Refresh button.

TIP   Double-click the column buttons at the top of the Microsoft Map Control to see the source for the data.

Maps: Adding Text Labels

You can add text labels with the size and font you want anywhere on your map. You also can edit existing labels that Excel supplied when you created the map. (See "Maps: Creating a Basic Data Map" before you complete this task.)

Steps

1. Double-click the map to activate it.

 2. Click the Add Text button on the Map toolbar.

3. Click the insertion point in the map where you want the text to appear and type the text; then press Enter.

4. Repeat step 3 for each additional label you want to add.

TIP   You can move text labels by dragging them anywhere in the map. To format a text label, right-click the text, choose Format Font from the shortcut menu, then make your formatting selections from the Font dialog box. To delete the text label, right-click it and then choose Clear.

Maps: Changing the Column Source

You can use the Microsoft Map Control to plot different columns of data and watch the map change. (See "Maps: Creating a Basic Data Map" before you complete this task.)

Steps

1. Double-click the map to activate it.

 2. If the Microsoft Map Control doesn't appear, click the Show/Hide Microsoft Map Control button on the Map toolbar.

3. Drag a column button from the top of the Microsoft Map Control down on top of a column button in the working area (the white box inside the Microsoft Map Control).

   The dropped column button replaces the column button in the working area, and the map redraws to show the new column of data.

 4. If necessary, click the Map Refresh button on the Map toolbar to update the map.

Maps: Creating a Basic Data Map

Excel enables you to easily create a geographical map based on data in your worksheet. The geographic identifiers (such as state abbreviation or country name) should appear in the first column, with data column(s) appearing to the right. Include the headings at the top of the data columns.

Why Use Maps?

You can use maps for many common business applications that involve geographical data. For example, you can create a map that shows how sales and commissions are distributed by region.

Maps Provided with Excel

The following geographical maps are provided in a standard installation of Excel: Australia, Canada, Europe, Mexico, Southern Africa, UK and ROI, United States (with AK & HI Inset), United States in North America, and World Countries.

If you are unable to access maps, a custom installation of Excel 97 that did not include map information may have been performed on your system to conserve disk space. In this case, you need to run Excel Setup again to install the maps.

The Data Map feature is an Excel add-in written by MapInfo Corporation. Although the maps and data that come with Excel may suit your needs, you also can purchase add-in maps, data, and feature extensions from MapInfo. These maps include census data and features such as roads, cities, and airports. For more information on how to contact MapInfo and purchase these items, activate a data map and choose Help, How to Get More Data.

NOTE When creating or modifying a data map, Excel displays the Microsoft Map menu and toolbar. These appear only when the map is active. ▓

Steps

1. In the worksheet, select the range containing the geographic identifiers and associated data that you want to map.

2. Click the Map button on the Standard toolbar, then drag across the area where you want the map to appear (make the map frame as large as possible). Release the mouse button.

3. If the Data Map feature cannot determine a unique map to use when it analyzes the left column of data, it displays the Multiple Maps Available dialog box. Select the map you want to use; then click OK to display the map.

4. Use the Microsoft Map Control dialog box to specify the column of data and which type of map you want. The gray buttons at the top of the dialog box represent the columns in your selected data range. The six buttons on the left side of the dialog box enable you to change the map type.

The default map created is a value shaded map using the first column of data. To change the data in the map, drag the column and format buttons you want to use into the white box inside the Microsoft Map Control.

5. Size and format the map if you want.

TIP To activate a map, double-click inside the map. A thick border appears around an activated map.

NOTE The data you plan to map must include geographical data, such as country, state, city, or county names; or postal codes. For more information on the types of data you can map and the abbreviations accepted by Excel, see the file named MAPSTATS.XLS. This worksheet also contains sample population sizes and forecasts you can experiment with. To find MAPSTATS.XLS on your computer, click the Start button, then choose Find, Files or Folders; then type the file name and click Find Now.

(See also "Maps: Entering Map Titles.")

Maps: Customizing Maps

You sometimes may use maps to show data at a certain point in time. You also may use maps as decision resources—they present information and plot data so the viewer can analyze the information and use it to support decisions. Excel provides a variety of symbols you can use to customize maps, so the viewer can better understand the differences in the data points.

You can customize each of the map formats to use different symbols, dots, and so forth. For example, you can change the color and symbols used with a graduated symbol format. Or you can change the dot density by specifying how many units each dot represents. (See "Maps: Creating a Basic Data Map" before you complete this task.)

Steps

1. Double-click the map to activate it.

2. From the Map menu, choose the appropriate Options command from the bottom of the menu. Commands for map formats appear on the menu only when that format is in use in the current map. Examples of these options include Category Shading Options, Value Shading Options, and Dot Density Options.

3. Each map format has a different dialog box and different set of options. Choose the options you want from the dialog box; then click OK.

TIP   A quick way to display the customizing options for a map format is to double-click the Map Format button that appears in the work area of the Microsoft Map Control.

Maps: Deleting a Map

You can delete an existing map if you no longer need the map or if you want to create an entirely new map in its place.

NOTE   You cannot delete a map when it is active. If the map is active (an active map has a thick border around it), select a cell in the worksheet to deactivate the map and then proceed with the following steps. ▓

Steps

1. Click the map once to select it. Handles appear around the map.

2. Press Delete.

Maps: Entering Map Titles

Your data map already includes a main title as soon as you create the map. This title appears in a bordered box at the top of the map. You also can add a subtitle to your map. (See "Maps: Creating a Basic Data Map" before you complete this task.)

Steps

1. Double-click the map to activate it.

2. Choose View, Subtitle. (If your map isn't showing a main title, choose View, Title if you want to display it.)

3. To edit the text in the subtitle (or the main title), select the title and then click where you want the insertion point.

4. Use standard Windows editing techniques to modify the text in the title. Press Enter to enter the title.

Maps: Formatting Map Titles

You can enhance the appearance of your map titles by changing the font, font styles, and font color used for the titles. (See "Maps: Creating a Basic Data Map" and "Maps: Entering Map Titles" before you complete this task.)

Steps

1. Double-click the map to activate it.

2. Right-click the title and choose Format Font from the shortcut menu.

3. Select the options you want to change in the Font dialog box, such as Font, Font Style, Size, and Color; then click OK.

TIP You can drag the title (or subtitle) to a new location by clicking the title one time and then dragging it by the border. To remove a title or subtitle, select it and then press the Delete key.

Maps: Inserting Data in an Existing Map

The Data Map feature enables you to easily add new data to your map. (See "Maps: Creating a Basic Data Map" before you complete this task.)

Steps

1. Select cells in the middle of the current data range; then, from the Insert menu, choose Cells.

CHARTS AND GRAPHICS

2. Choose the Shift Cells Down option; then click OK.

3. Enter the new region name and data where you inserted the cells.

4. Double-click the map to reactivate it; then click the Map Refresh button on the toolbar to update the map.

Maps: Refreshing a Map

When you make changes to worksheet data that your map uses, you need to refresh the map so it reflects these changes. Excel may not automatically update the map as you edit worksheet data. When you need to update the map, the Map Refresh button on the Map toolbar becomes available.

Steps

1. Double-click the map to activate it.

2. Click the Map Refresh button on the Map toolbar. If this button appears gray, the map has already been refreshed.

 TIP To change the map refresh from manual to automatic, activate the map and choose Tools, Options. Then choose Automatic and click OK.

Maps: Zooming in a Data Map

Data maps cover a great deal of geographic area, but you may be interested only in a few states or countries. You can magnify maps and reposition them so that they show only the area in which you are interested. (See "Maps: Creating a Basic Data Map" before you complete this task.)

Steps

1. Double-click the map to activate it.

2. Click the Zoom Percentage of Map drop-down list on the Map toolbar; then select or type a magnification.

3. Press Enter or click the map to see the map magnify. To return to the default size, click the Display Entire button on the Map toolbar.

4. If you want to move the magnified map within the map window, click the Grabber button on the Map toolbar and drag the map. To return to the previous view of your map, choose <u>V</u>iew, <u>P</u>revious.

TIP   If you prefer a magnification different from the values in the list, type a magnification. To increase magnification greater than the default, enter a number greater than 100 percent. To decrease magnification, enter a number less than 100 percent.

TROUBLESHOOTING   **After zooming in on a data map, the map seems to have disappeared. How do I get it back?** You probably zoomed in on a blank area of the map. Click the Display Entire button on the Map toolbar to show the entire map. Then try the zoom procedure again.

Saving Charts

To save a chart that is embedded in a worksheet or that appears as a separate sheet in the workbook, you save the workbook that contains the worksheet.

Steps

1. Modify the chart as you want.

2. Click the Save button on the Standard toolbar.

3. If the Save As dialog box appears, type a name for the workbook that contains the chart, then click <u>S</u>ave.

NOTE   When you format and enhance a chart in Excel 97 and save it as an earlier version file, you may lose some of the formatting or enhancements. This is due to incompatibilities between Excel 97 and earlier versions of Excel. ■

Customizing

You can customize Excel in a number of ways to suit your needs. You can have Excel display certain workbooks when it starts. In addition, you can choose to display formulas instead of the results of the formulas. You also can hide (and unhide) an entire workbook, worksheets within a workbook, and row and column headings.

Excel enables you to move, resize, and customize on-screen menus and toolbars. You also can record macros that duplicate common keystrokes; you can even assign a macro to a toolbar button. If you create workbooks used by others, you can create a template that contains all the necessary data, formulas, macros, and formatting.

In Excel, you can use many different methods to adjust the display of windows, or adjust how you view data in your workbooks. You can freeze the worksheet pane in large worksheets, for example, so that row and column headings always remain on-screen. You also can zoom the display and move or size windows.

Changing International Character Sets

In Windows, you can switch among different international character sets, time and date displays, and numeric formats. The international settings you choose show up in the formatting in your Excel worksheets and in other Windows applications. When you choose Format, Cells in Excel, for example, the Number tab shows number and date/time formats for the country or regions you have selected in the Windows Control Panel.

The Regional Settings Properties dialog box enables you to change the country, language, date, currency, and other formats. Changes to these settings aren't permanent—you can change them again at any time.

Steps

1. To choose the international settings you want to use, click the Start button on the Windows taskbar and then choose Settings, Control Panel. Double-click the Regional Settings icon.

2. To automatically change the settings for the Number, Currency, Time, and Date tabs to those used in a particular region, select the region you want from the drop-down list in the Regional Settings tab. Or, to change the number, currency, time or date formats individually, click the appropriate tab and select the formats you want to use.

3. Click OK when you have finished. The settings you chose take effect in all your Windows applications that use these settings.

Creating a Custom Color

Excel uses a palette of 56 colors—40 colors for worksheets and 16 colors for charts. You can change the palette colors used in the current workbook. After you define a set of colors, you can then copy those colors to other workbooks.

You can change the colors in a color palette in two ways. You can select new colors from a grid of standard colors, using the Standard tab of the Colors dialog box; or you can create your own custom colors, using the Custom tab in the Colors dialog box.

Steps

1. Open the workbook in which you want to use custom colors. Choose Tools, Options; then click the Color tab.

2. Select the color in the palette that you want to change by clicking a color box.

3. Click the <u>M</u>odify button to display the Colors dialog box. Click the Standard tab and select the desired color you want to use from the <u>C</u>olors grid.

4. If you don't see the exact color you want on the Standard tab, click the Custom tab to create your own color. In the <u>C</u>olors box, click on the color you want. A preview of the color appears in the New box.

5. When you have finished selecting your color, click OK twice to accept the color and return to the worksheet.

To fine-tune a color, use the text boxes below the <u>C</u>olors box. Each text box includes a number from 0 to 255. H<u>u</u>e is the actual color itself; <u>S</u>at (saturation) is the color intensity; <u>L</u>um (luminosity) is the color brightness; <u>R</u>ed, <u>G</u>reen, and <u>B</u>lue indicate the level each of these colors contributes to the overall color. Drag the slider beside the <u>C</u>olors box to adjust the luminosity of the selected color. To return the palette to its original set of 56 colors, click the <u>R</u>eset button on the Color tab.

To copy a color palette from one workbook to another, open both workbooks and activate the workbook that will receive the new palette. Choose <u>T</u>ools, <u>O</u>ptions; then click the Color tab. In the <u>C</u>opy Colors From list box, select the name of the workbook from which you are copying colors; then click OK. Existing colored objects in the workbook receiving the new palette automatically change to reflect the new palette.

(See also "Colors and Patterns" in the "Formatting" section.)

Displaying: A Worksheet Full Screen

In the normal worksheet view, screen elements such as the title bar, toolbars, the formula bar, and the status bar take up on-screen space. Excel enables you to switch the display to a full-screen view, in which only the worksheet is displayed along with the menu bar and sheet tabs. This enables you to see more data in the worksheet on-screen at one time. You can switch between these views at any time.

CUSTOMIZING

Steps

1. With a worksheet open, choose View, Full Screen. The worksheet display changes to full-screen view.

2. To return to normal view, click the Close Full Screen button that appears below the worksheet.

You can add one or more toolbars to the full-screen view by choosing the View, Toolbars command and selecting the toolbar you want to display.

 TIP To hide or display screen elements, choose Tools, Options; then click the View tab and make the desired selections.

(See also "Zooming: The Worksheet Display.")

Displaying: Worksheets in Separate Windows

In the default workbook view, you only see one worksheet at a time in the workbook's window. When you click a sheet tab to display a different worksheet, that worksheet then displays using the entire workbook window. Excel enables you to display multiple worksheets in separate windows if you want to see them on-screen at one time.

Steps

1. Open only the workbook containing the worksheets you want to display in multiple windows.

2. Choose Window, New Window once for each additional worksheet you want to see. This opens a new workbook window each time you choose the command.

3. Choose Window, Arrange.

4. Select the option you want to use to arrange the windows on-screen: Tiled, Horizontal, Vertical, or Cascade; then click OK.

5. The workbooks now appear in separate windows on-screen. To see different worksheets in the additional workbooks you added, click the window to activate it,

and then click the sheet tab for the worksheet you want to see.

(See also "Windows: Moving or Sizing.")

Hiding: Gridlines

You can hide the worksheet gridlines (and other screen elements) to make the display appear less like a spreadsheet and more like a graphic or paper display. Hiding the on-screen gridlines also gives a better appearance to data-entry forms and on-screen reports. You may want to display the gridlines while you build formulas or place text boxes and objects in a worksheet.

Steps

1. To turn the worksheet gridlines off, choose Tools, Options; then click the View tab.

2. Clear the Gridlines check box.

TIP   If you want to change the color of the on-screen gridlines, choose Tools, Options; then click the View tab. Ensure that the Gridlines check box is selected and select a color from the Color drop-down list; then click OK.

NOTE   Do not confuse the display of gridlines in the worksheet on-screen with printed gridlines. The Gridlines check box in the Page Setup dialog box controls the printing of gridlines. ■

(See also "Printing: Worksheet Gridlines" in the "Producing Output" section.)

Hiding: Row and Column Headings

If you are working with a small number of rows and columns, you may not need to refer to the column and row headings (sometimes referred to as the *worksheet frame*) as you work. You may also choose to remove these headings from the screen to increase the visible workspace on-screen, or to make the screen appear less cluttered when giving an on-screen presentation.

Steps

1. With a worksheet open, choose Tools, Options; then click the View tab.

2. In the Window Options area, clear the Row & Column Headers check box.

NOTE There are other parts of the Excel worksheet that you can hide from view. Some of these options appear on the View tab when you choose Tools, Options. For example, you can hide the Formula Bar, the Status Bar, the Sheet Tabs, and the Horizontal or Vertical scroll bars. ■

Hiding: Workbooks

Workbooks can become quite cluttered as you work with them. To simplify your workspace, you can hide an entire workbook window. If only one workbook is open in Excel, when you hide the window, the entire workbook is hidden. (See also "Hiding: Worksheets.")

Steps

1. Place the mouse pointer in the workbook you want to hide.

2. Choose Window, Hide.

If you need to modify or view a hidden workbook, you will first need to restore the workbook. Choose Window, Unhide. In the Unhide dialog box, select the name of the workbook you want to display; then click OK.

> **CAUTION** When you hide a workbook, it remains hidden after you quit Excel and then try to open the workbook again. If you will not be using your workbook for some time, or if others need to access the same workbook, you may forget that you have hidden the workbook. You should therefore remember to unhide workbooks each time you exit Excel.

(See also "Protecting: Workbooks" in the section "Editing Workbooks.")

Hiding: Worksheets

You may want to hide only selected worksheets in a workbook. Perhaps you have three worksheets and want to work with just two of them, or you may want to hide a worksheet in a shared workbook so that others will not see the worksheet. (See also "Hiding: Workbooks.")

Steps

1. Click the sheet tab for the worksheet you want to hide.

2. Choose Format, Sheet, Hide.

If you need to modify or view a hidden worksheet, you will first need to restore the worksheet. Choose Format, Sheet, Unhide. In the Unhide dialog box, select the name of the worksheet you want to display; then click OK.

> **TIP** You can hide more than one worksheet in a workbook. Click the first sheet tab, then hold down Ctrl and click the other sheets you want to hide. Then follow the steps above to hide the selected worksheets.

> **NOTE** If your workbook includes just one worksheet, you cannot hide that worksheet. To get around this problem, insert a new, blank worksheet in your workbook; then hide the other worksheet. ■

(See also "Protecting: Individual Worksheets" in the section "Editing Workbooks.")

Macros: Attaching to Buttons

You can attach *macros* you create in Excel to a button control on a worksheet. This feature enables you to run a macro with the click of a single button. You can attach macros to buttons if you create data-entry forms used by others, for example; then they can just click the button to run a simple to complex macro procedure. Some of Excel's predefined templates include button controls with macros attached to them. (See "Macros: Recording Macros" before you complete this task.)

Steps

1. Display the Forms toolbar by right-clicking in the toolbar area and choosing Forms.

 2. Click the Button tool on the Forms toolbar. The pointer changes to a crosshair.

3. Click and drag to draw a button on the worksheet. You can later size or move the button, if necessary.

4. The Assign Macro dialog box appears when you release the mouse button. Select the macro you want to assign to the control; then click OK.

5. Click outside the button to deselect it. To run the macro assigned to the button, click the button.

Hold down Ctrl and then click the button to select it. When a button is selected, handles appear around the object. You can then move, resize, or change the properties of the button. Drag an edge of the button to move it. Resize the button by dragging one of the handles. Delete the button by pressing Delete. Click outside the button to deselect it.

 TIP To change the name displayed on the button, hold down Ctrl and then click the button. Use the normal editing keys to edit the text in the button.

(See also "Forms: Adding Controls" in the section "Data Analysis.")

Macros: Enabling Virus Protection

To help prevent *macros* from corrupting your system, Excel provides a feature that checks each workbook you open for the existence of macros (some Excel viruses are started from macros). If a workbook contains one or more macros, Excel displays a warning message notifying you of this. If you see this message, you should only continue to open the workbook if you trust the source from which you obtained the workbook. This message is only an indication that the workbook contains macros; Excel is not able to check whether or not the macros actually contain viruses, or if there are any other viruses associated with that workbook (not related to macros).

NOTE You can purchase antivirus software that scans your workbooks and removes known macro viruses. To obtain information on this software, access Microsoft's Web site (**http//:www.microsoft.com**) and search on "virus."

Steps

1. With a workbook open, choose Tools, Options; then click the General tab.

2. Select the Macro Virus Protection check box; then click OK.

Macros: Recording Macros

If you find yourself performing tedious, repetitive actions over and over again in your worksheets, you can automate the task by creating a macro. A *macro* is a stored list of commands and keystrokes that are automatically executed by Excel. You use Excel's Record feature to record the actions you perform, and then store these recorded keystrokes as the macro. The next time you need to perform the action, you can run the macro.

CUSTOMIZING

Steps

1. Choose Tools, Macro, Record Macro; in the Macro Name text box, type a name for the macro.

2. If you want to assign a shortcut key to the macro, type a letter in the Shortcut Key text box. (You can later press Ctrl+*letter* to run the macro. If you press Shift as you type the letter in the text box, you later press Shift+Ctrl+*letter* to run the macro.)

3. In the Store Macro In box, select the location where you want to store the macro. If you want a macro to be available whenever you use Excel, select the Personal Macro Workbook option.

4. Click OK; then perform the actions you want the macro to record, in the order you want them to occur.

 5. Click the Stop Recording button when you have finished.

Macros: Running Macros

After you have created a *macro*, you then run the macro to execute the commands. You can run a macro from the Tools menu, from an assigned shortcut key combination (if you assigned one to the macro), or from a macro button (if you attached the macro to a button). (See "Macros: Recording Macros" before you complete this task.)

Steps

1. Open the workbook in which you want to run the macro; if necessary, move the cell pointer to an appropriate location.

2. Choose Tools, Macro, Macros.

3. In the list box, select the macro you want to run; then click Run to run the macro.

If you did not assign a macro to a shortcut key when you created the macro, you can assign it later. Choose Tools, Macro, Macros; select the macro name and click the Options button. Type a letter in the Shortcut Key text box; then click OK. To run the macro using the shortcut key, press Ctrl+*letter*. If you pressed Shift when you typed the letter in the text box, you must press Shift+Ctrl+*letter* to run the macro.

To run a macro you assigned to a button control on the worksheet, click the button.

(See also "Macros: Attaching to Buttons.")

Macros: Viewing Macro Code

After you record a *macro*, you can view the macro code in the Visual Basic Editor and modify the macro, as necessary. If you aren't very familiar with Visual Basic, the language Excel uses to record macros, you may want to experiment with creating macros that perform different types of tasks. You then can view the code to see how your actions translate to Visual Basic. This may make it easier for you to understand how to edit the macro, if that becomes necessary. (See "Macros: Recording Macros" before you complete this task.)

Steps

1. With Excel open, choose Tools, Macro, Macros.

2. Select the macro you want to view (or edit) in the list box; then click the Edit button.

3. The macro code appears in a window in the Visual Basic Editor; view the macro and edit it, as necessary (or you can record the macro again, if you prefer).

4. To return to the worksheet, choose File, Close and Return to Microsoft Excel. Any changes you made to the macro are automatically saved.

Menus: Adding Commands to Menus

Excel includes many more commands than you would ever want to place on a menu at one time. You might want to add the commands you use most often onto an existing or custom menu, however. You can add any command to a menu that you want to have easy access to. As with toolbar buttons, when you

CUSTOMIZING

add commands to a menu, they are available in any workbook. You can always remove commands you added to a menu, or use a reset command to revert the menu to Excel's default menu.

Steps

1. Choose Tools, Customize; then click the Commands tab.

2. Click the menu on the menu bar that you want to modify. In the Categories list box, select the category for the command.

3. Select the specific command you want to add to the menu from the Commands list box; then drag and drop the command onto the desired menu location and release the mouse button. The new menu item appears on the menu.

4. Click the Close button to close the Customize dialog box.

To remove a new command from a menu, choose Tools, Customize; then click the Commands tab. Display the menu in the workbook that contains the added command; then drag the command off the menu to remove it. Click Close to close the Customize dialog box.

If you added multiple commands to a menu, or you aren't sure exactly what changes you made to a menu, or you think you deleted an Excel menu item by mistake, you can easily reset the menu back to Excel's defaults. Choose Tools, Customize; then click the Commands tab. Display the menu in the workbook that you want to reset; then click the Modify Selection button in the Customize dialog box, and click the Reset option. Click Close to close the Customize dialog box.

Menus: Moving the Menu

In Excel 97, you can move the menu bar to display anywhere on the screen—on any edge of the screen or as a floating menu bar inside the worksheet area. This works in a similar way to moving toolbars. In most cases, however, you will probably

want to keep the menu docked to the top of the worksheet, just
below the title bar.

Steps

1. Point to a gray area inside the menu bar.

2. Drag the menu bar to the desired location and then
   release the mouse button.

To move the menu back to its original location, drag the menu
and drop it just below the title bar.

Moving the Active Cell after Data Entry

By default, Excel moves the active cell down one cell after you
type data in a cell and press Enter. If you type data in cell B2
and press Enter, for example, cell B3 becomes the next active
cell; if you then type an entry in cell B3 and press Enter, then
cell B4 becomes the active cell, and so on. You can change this
option so that the active cell is one cell up, down, or to the left.
If you deselect the option, the pointer stays in the same cell
when you press Enter.

Steps

1. With a workbook open, choose Tools, Options; then click
   the Edit tab.

2. Ensure that the Move Selection after Enter check box is
   selected.

3. In the Direction drop-down list, select the direction you
   want to move the active cell after you type data in a cell
   and press Enter; then click OK.

Naming and Saving a Custom View

If you have customized the worksheet view and want to save
the view settings so that you can later return to them, you can
create a custom view. Custom views save settings such as
hidden rows or columns, filter settings, and print settings. (See
also "Displaying: A Worksheet Full Screen.")

Steps

1. Set up the workbook with the view you want to save, and choose View, Custom Views; then click the Add button.

2. Type a name for the view in the Name box; then click OK.

 TIP To later access the custom view, choose View, Custom Views; then select the name of the view in the Views list box and click Show.

Startup: Controlling Excel's Startup

If you use the same Excel workbook every day, such as a sales data workbook, you can place that workbook on the Windows 95 Start menu. Then, when you click the workbook icon on the Start menu, both Excel and the workbook open automatically.

Steps

1. Open Windows Explorer, and find the workbook you want to open each time you start Excel.

2. Drag the icon to the Start Menu folder (normally located in the Windows folder).

3. Windows 95 places an icon for the workbook on the Start menu. Click the icon to start Excel with your workbook open.

(See also "Startup: Setting Startup Switches.")

Startup: Setting Startup Switches

You can set a number of switches to control how Excel starts. For instance, you might not want to see the Excel startup screen and a new, blank workbook each time. For information on all the available startup switches in Excel, search on "switches" in the Excel on-line Help.

Steps

1. In Windows Explorer, find the Microsoft Excel shortcut icon (open the Windows folder, then open the Start Menu folder and click the Programs folder.)

2. Right-click the Microsoft Excel icon, and then click Properties.

3. Click the Shortcut tab.

4. In the Target text box, place the insertion point after the path to Microsoft Excel, type a space, and then type the switch you want to use. If you type /e, for example, the startup screen and blank workbook won't display.

5. Click OK to close the Properties dialog box.

(See also "Startup: Controlling Excel's Startup.")

Templates: Creating and Using a Workbook Template

In addition to creating new, blank workbook files, you can also create new workbooks from templates. Excel provides a variety of predefined template files, ranging in functionality from business worksheets to personal financial templates. (See also "Template Wizard: Using Excel's Templates" in the section "Data Analysis.")

If one of Excel's predefined templates doesn't meet your needs, however, you can easily create your own custom template. Template files can contain all the data, formulas, macros, and formatting you need. This enables you to quickly get to work, rather than re-creating this information from scratch when you need it.

Steps

1. Open a workbook and display the worksheet you want to save as a template. Enter and format all the data you want to include with the template, as desired.

2. Choose File, Save As, and in the File Name box, type the name you want to use for the new template.

3. In the Save as Type drop-down list, select Template. The default folder automatically changes to the Templates folder.

CUSTOMIZING

4. Click Save to save the template with the new name in the specified folder.

5. To enter data using the template you created, choose File, New to create a new workbook based on the template. The new workbook contains all the formatting, formulas, and data contained in the template, but it must be saved using a different name.

Templates: Editing Templates

You can edit existing templates at any time if you need to change text, formatting, or any other elements in the template. You can then save the template using the same name or save it as a different template. In addition to editing your own work-book templates, you also can edit Excel's predefined templates. (See "Templates: Creating and Using a Workbook Template" before you complete this task.)

Steps

1. Choose File, Open, and in the Files of Type drop-down list, select Templates. If necessary, change the folder in the Look In list.

2. Select the template name in the list window; then click Open. If there are macros in the template, a warning dialog box appears; if this happens, click Enable Macros to open the template.

3. Make the desired changes to the template.

4. To save the template using the same name, choose File, Save. Or, to save the template using a different name, choose File, Save As, type the new file name in File Name box, and click Save.

 TIP To delete a template, select it in the Open dialog box and press the Delete key. Then click Yes to confirm the deletion, and click Cancel to close the Open dialog box.

NOTE Changes made to templates only affect workbooks and worksheets that are created after the template used to create the new workbooks is modified. Existing workbooks are not changed when you edit a template on which they are based. ▪

Toolbars: Adding Toolbar Buttons

If you frequently use a command that is not represented on an Excel toolbar, you can easily add a button that performs the command to the toolbar. If you often format cells with light shading, for example, you can add the Light Shading button to the Formatting toolbar. If there is not room to add a button to an existing toolbar, you can remove an existing button that you don't use on a toolbar, or you can create a new toolbar. (See also "Toolbars: Creating a New Toolbar.")

Steps

1. Display the toolbar that you want to add a button to, if necessary.

2. Choose Tools, Customize; then click the Commands tab.

3. In the Categories list box, select the category that includes the command you want the button to perform.

4. Find the button you want in the Commands list, and then drag that button to the displayed toolbar, where you want the toolbar button to appear. Release the mouse button.

5. Click Close to close the Customize dialog box.

 TIP To remove a button from a toolbar, display the toolbar that includes the button you want to remove. Choose Tools, Customize; then click the Commands tab. Drag the button off the toolbar; then click Close.

 TIP To reset a toolbar to its original configuration, choose Tools, Customize; then click the Toolbars tab. Select the toolbar you want to reset, and then click the Reset button. Click OK to confirm the procedure; then click Close to close the dialog box.

CUSTOMIZING

Toolbars: Changing the Button Image

You can use the Button Editor to change the appearance of an image on a toolbar button, pixel by pixel. Or, you can choose from a pop-up list of over 40 predefined images that Excel provides.

Steps

1. Display the toolbar containing the button whose image you want to change.

2. Choose Tools, Customize. Right-click the toolbar button you want to change; then choose Edit Button Image from the menu. The Button Editor appears.

3. In the Picture area, you see a representation of the button's picture; each square of the picture is a pixel. If you want to create a picture from scratch, click the Clear button. To change the color of the pixels and create the button image, click a color in the Colors area, and then click the pixel you want to change to that color. Use the buttons in the Move area if you want to move the entire picture up, down, left, or right. The button in the Preview area shows you what the button will look like in the standard button size.

4. When you have finished creating the new button image, click OK. The button in the toolbar now contains the new image. Click Close to close the Customize dialog box.

 TIP To use one of the predefined button images that Excel provides, display the toolbar containing the button whose image you want to change. Choose Tools, Customize. Right-click the toolbar button you want to change; then highlight the Change Button Image option. If you see an image you like, click the image. The button changes to display the new image. Click Close to close the Customize dialog box.

Toolbars: Creating a New Toolbar

Although you can add individual buttons to Excel's existing toolbars, you may find that you want to create your own custom toolbar with multiple buttons used for specific tasks that you frequently perform. If you use a workbook that has unique formatting and printing requirements, for example, you can create a new toolbar with just those buttons related to formatting and printing that workbook. You also may want to create a new toolbar for use with custom templates you create. After you create a new toolbar, you can move or resize it just as you can move or resize Excel's predefined toolbars. (See also "Toolbars: Displaying or Hiding," "Toolbars: Adding Toolbar Buttons," and "Templates: Creating and Using a Workbook Template.")

Steps

1. Choose Tools, Customize; then click the Toolbars tab.

2. Click the New button. In the Toolbar Name text box, type a name for the toolbar; then click OK.

3. To add buttons to the new toolbar, click the Commands tab in the Customize dialog box.

4. In the Categories list box, select the category that includes the command you want the button to perform. Find the button you want in the Commands list, and then drag that button to the new toolbar. Release the mouse button.

5. Repeat Step 4 above for each additional button you want to add to the new toolbar. When you have finished, click Close.

TIP   If you want a custom toolbar to be available with a specific workbook, you can attach it to that workbook. Open the workbook, display the custom toolbar, and choose Tools, Customize; then click the Toolbars tab. Click the Attach button. In the Custom Toolbars list, select the toolbar you want to attach; then click the Copy button. Click OK and then click Close to return to the workbook.

CUSTOMIZING

Toolbars: Displaying or Hiding

When you start Excel, the Standard and Formatting toolbars appear on-screen by default. You will use these toolbars most often when you work in Excel. Excel also offers several additional toolbars you can display when you need them. Sometimes, different toolbars will automatically appear on-screen when you are performing certain procedures. When you create a pivot table, for example, the PivotTable toolbar appears on-screen. Toolbars that are currently on-screen display with check marks beside their name in the View, Toolbars menu.

Steps

- To display another toolbar, choose View, Toolbars; then click the name of the toolbar you want to display.

- To hide a toolbar that currently appears on-screen, choose View, Toolbars; then click the name of the toolbar you want to hide.

 TIP If the toolbar is a floating toolbar, you can hide the toolbar by clicking the Close button in the toolbar's title bar.

(See also "Toolbars: Moving and Resizing.")

Toolbars: Moving and Resizing

By default, the Standard and Formatting toolbars appear at the top of the screen, just below the title bar. You can move any toolbar so that it is attached to any edge of the screen or floating inside the workbook. Toolbars attached to an edge of the window are sometimes referred to as docked toolbars. If an on-screen toolbar is not docked, it is floating. Floating toolbars can be resized.

Steps

- To move a docked toolbar, click the move handle (the double vertical lines at the left side of the toolbar) and drag the toolbar where you want it to appear.

■ To move a floating toolbar, click the title bar of the toolbar and drag the toolbar where you want it to appear.

■ To resize a floating toolbar, point to an edge of the toolbar (the mouse pointer becomes a double-sided arrow), and then drag in the direction you want to size the toolbar.

(See also "Toolbars: Displaying or Hiding.")

Windows: Freezing Worksheet Panes

When working in large worksheets, the worksheet headings typically scroll from the screen as you move through the worksheet. Excel enables you to freeze the window pane at selected rows and columns so that they remain on-screen as you scroll through large worksheets. (See also "Windows: Splitting Worksheet Windows.")

Steps

1. Position the cell pointer at the intersection of the row and column that you want to remain on-screen when you move through the worksheet.

2. Choose Window, Freeze Panes.

To unfreeze the window pane, choose Window, Unfreeze Panes.

Windows: Minimizing, Maximizing, and Restoring

To obtain more space on your computer screen if it has become cluttered, you can store open applications or workbook windows by minimizing them so that they become buttons in the Windows taskbar at the bottom of the screen. When you need one of the applications or workbooks that has been minimized, you can restore the icon to its former window location and size. If you want a window to fill the entire available display area, you can maximize it.

CUSTOMIZING

To perform these procedures, you use the Minimize and Maximize/Restore icons located on the right end of a window's title bar (just beside the Close icon). When you click a Maximize icon to maximize a window, the icon changes to a Restore icon, and vice versa.

Steps

■ To maximize an application or workbook window using the mouse, click the Maximize icon for the active window. (The Maximize icon is located just to the left of the Close icon.)

■ To minimize an application or workbook window so that it is stored temporarily at the bottom of the screen, click the Minimize icon. (The Minimize icon is located just left of the Maximize/Restore icon.)

■ If the application or workbook has been minimized to a button at the bottom of the screen, click the button to restore it. Or, if the application or workbook is maximized, click the Restore icon to restore it to its earlier window size. (The Restore icon is located just to the left of the Close icon.)

 TIP To switch between open workbook windows, choose Window; then select the window you want to display from the bottom of the Window menu.

Windows: Moving or Sizing

With multiple workbooks on-screen, you will occasionally want to move workbook windows out of the way if they are obstructing data or other windows you want to see. You also can resize a window so that it takes up less (or more) space on-screen. You can only move or size a window if it is not maximized. (See also "Windows: Minimizing, Maximizing, and Restoring.")

Steps

■ To move a window, select the window you want to move. Drag the title bar until the shadow outline is where you want the window to appear; then release the mouse button.

- To resize a window, drag the window edge or corner to the location you want; then release the mouse button.

(See also "Displaying: Worksheets in Separate Windows.")

Windows: Splitting Worksheet Windows

In addition to freezing worksheet panes, Excel also enables you to split a worksheet in two, allowing you to view two different areas of one worksheet at the same time. When you split a worksheet, additional scroll bars appear, which you can use to scroll areas independently of one another. (See also "Windows: Freezing Worksheet Panes.")

Steps

- To split the worksheet horizontally, select the first cell in the row where you want to split the worksheet. Then choose Window, Split.

- To split the worksheet vertically, select the first cell in the column where you want to split the worksheet. Then choose Window, Split.

- To remove the split, choose Window, Remove Split.

TIP   You can drag the split bar to view a larger portion of one worksheet area.

Zooming: The Worksheet Display

Excel provides many options for viewing your worksheets. In addition to customizing the view and specifying which on-screen elements are displayed, you can zoom the worksheet to a percentage you specify. The default zoom percentage in a new worksheet is 100%, but you can change the zoom percentage to between 10% and 400%. Choose a percentage larger than 100% to zoom in on a worksheet and display enlarged text, or less than 100% to reduce the size of the displayed text and see more data on-screen.

Steps

1. With a worksheet open, choose <u>V</u>iew, <u>Z</u>oom. The Zoom dialog box appears.

2. In the Magnification area, select the zoom percentage you want to use; then click OK. The worksheet display changes to the zoom percentage you selected.

TIP   You also can use the Zoom control in the Standard toolbar to change the magnification. Click the arrow beside the control and select the option you want; or, to enter a custom percent, click the control, type the zoom percentage, and then press Enter.

(See also "Displaying: A Worksheet Full Screen" in this section and "Microsoft IntelliMouse: Zooming" in the section "Getting Started.")

Data Analysis

One of the fundamental uses of a spreadsheet program is to analyze data. Excel provides multiple tools for making analysis easier for novice Excel users, as well as more complex tools for engineers, scientists, and financial analysts.

You can use Excel to create databases or lists of information. Features such as the Data Form enable you to quickly insert, delete, and search database records. You also can easily sort and filter data in a database. Using the outlining or pivot table features, you can manipulate lists to summarize data by using different views . You can use Goal Seek and Solver to find answers to financial problems that require an optimum solution.

Excel's AutoFill, AutoComplete, and Pick From List features enable you to enter data more quickly. You can even use the Template Wizard to create your own professional-looking data entry forms that make it easier for others to enter data. These forms can include controls such as check boxes, scroll bars, and option buttons similar to those used in Excel dialog boxes.

AutoFill: Entering Custom Data Series

Excel enables you to create and insert a custom list or data series in a worksheet. Suppose that you frequently enter the same company department names in different worksheets. You can define these names as a list, enter the first name, and then have Excel's AutoFill feature fill in the remaining names. (See also "Entering: Data Series" in the section "Getting Started.")

Steps

1. With a worksheet open, choose <u>T</u>ools, <u>O</u>ptions; then click the Custom Lists tab.

2. In the List <u>E</u>ntries box, type the entries you want to include in the custom list. Press Enter after each entry.

3. Click <u>A</u>dd. The list you entered now appears in the Custom <u>L</u>ists box.

4. If you want to create additional custom lists, click NEW LIST in the Custom <u>L</u>ists box, and then repeat Steps 2 and 3 above.

5. Click OK to add the list and close the dialog box.

 TIP If you want to create a custom list based on existing text in a worksheet, use the <u>I</u>mport List From Cells text box to enter the range containing the list. Then click the Import button to import the list into the dialog box.

AutoFilter: Filtering a Database

The *AutoFilter* feature enables you to filter, or work with a subset of data in a list, without moving or sorting the list. Each field name at the top of the list becomes a drop-down list, from which you can choose which data you want to view. This feature allows you to easily perform editing and formatting commands on the resulting subset of data. (See "Databases: Creating a Database" before you complete this task.)

Available Filter Options

Options that are available for displaying data are listed in the following table:

AutoFilter Options	
Option	**Description**
(All)	Displays all records in this field (the default option).
(Top 10)	Enables you to filter a specified amount of numeric data from the top or bottom of a list.

Option	Description
(Custom)	Displays the Custom AutoFilter dialog box, enabling you to create AND or OR criteria.
(*Exact value*)	Displays only records with the exact value you specify in this field.
(Blanks)	Displays all records with blanks in this field.
(NonBlanks)	Displays all records with nonblanks (records that contain data) in this field.

Steps

1. Select any cell in the list; then choose Data, Filter, AutoFilter.

2. Click the drop-down list in the column that contains the data you want to filter.

3. Select the criteria you want to display for that field. Select from the options shown in the table above. As soon as you make an AutoFilter selection from a drop-down list, the worksheet hides rows that do not meet your criteria. You immediately see the results of your filter.

4. To discontinue AutoFilter for this list, choose Data, Filter, AutoFilter. The drop-down lists disappear from the field labels.

NOTE Data stored to the left or right of the list may be hidden when you filter the list. If other data shares the worksheet with the list, store it in rows above or below the list area. ■

Comments: Adding to a Cell

When you share a worksheet with other users, or if the data you use in a formula changes on a regular basis, you can attach a comment to a cell. Comments are descriptive notes commonly used to explain the data in a particular cell. These comments appear in pop-up text boxes when you move the pointer over the cell containing the comment.

Each comment automatically includes the author's name. Examples of items you may choose to include in a comment are: the date a worksheet (or cell) was last modified, worksheet assumptions, data-entry limits, the significance of a particular value, or the origin of a formula.

Steps

1. Select the cell you want to contain the comment, and choose Insert, Comment. You see a pop-up text box with your name.

2. Type the text for the comment; if you need to move to a new line, press Enter. Click in the worksheet area when you are finished.

3. To see the comment, point to the cell with the red indicator in the top right corner.

TIP If you frequently use the Auditing toolbar, you may prefer to use the New Comment button on the Auditing toolbar to add comments to the worksheet. To display the Auditing toolbar, choose Tools, Auditing, Show Auditing Toolbar.

NOTE To turn the comment indicator on or off, choose Tools, Options; then click the View tab. In the Comments area, select None to turn off the indicators, Comment Indicator Only to show just the indicator, or Comment & Indicator to show both the indicator and the comment. ■

(See also "Comments: Selecting, Finding, Editing, and Printing.")

Comments: Selecting, Finding, Editing, and Printing

After you've attached a comment to a cell in the worksheet, you can easily select worksheet comments, find specific text in comments, edit a comment, or print comments. (See "Comments: Adding to a Cell" before you complete this task.)

Steps

1. To select all the cells in a worksheet that contain comments, choose Edit, Go To; then click Special. Click the Comments option and click OK. You can then move between the selected cells by pressing Tab or Shift+Tab.

2. To search for specific text in worksheet comments, choose Edit, Find, and type the text in the Find What text box. In the Look In list, select Comments; then click Find Next. Click Close to close the dialog box.

3. To edit a comment, select the cell and choose Insert, Edit Comment. Edit the comment as you normally edit text in Excel. Click outside the text box when you are finished.

4. If you type more text than will fit within the text box, you can resize it. To do so, drag any of the selection handles.

5. To print the comments in a worksheet, choose File, Page Setup; then click the Sheet tab. Select Comments, and then choose whether you want to print the comments at the end of the sheet or as displayed in the sheet. Click Print to begin printing.

TIP To delete a comment, right-click the cell that contains the red indicator. Then choose Delete Comment from the shortcut menu.

Databases: Creating a Database

One of the most common uses of Excel is to help manage a *database.* You can use Excel database features to work with a simple *list* of information, such as a To Do list, or a larger, more complex database that contains several columns of data. In Excel, the terms *database* and *list* are often used interchangeably. This book uses the term *database* to refer to both simple lists and more complex databases.

A database includes information that contains similar sets of data, such as a client database. In an Excel database, the information in one row (such as all the information for one client) is known as a *record*. In each row, individual items are stored in *fields*—each field is a column in the database. An example of a field in a client database would be the client's name; another would be the address of the client. When information is organized in a database format, you can easily sort, filter, and summarize data.

Steps

1. Type the field names in a single row of a worksheet. These field names (such as Name, Address, Phone, and so on) will appear as column headers in your database.

2. Select all the field names and apply a style to them, such as boldface, italic, or a larger type font. This will make the field names stand out from the records of your database.

3. Type the records of your database (such as information on each client) directly below the field names, one record per row. Do not leave a blank row after the field names.

NOTE Your Excel database is actually just a special type of Excel worksheet. You can still use all the familiar worksheet commands to edit and format your database. ■

(See also "Databases: Inserting Records.")

Databases: Deleting Records

When you need to delete records from a database, you can delete them directly from the worksheet, or you can use a *data form* to locate and delete specific records. (See "Databases: Creating a Database" before you complete this task.)

Steps

1. To delete a record using the data form, select any cell in the database; then choose Data, Form.

2. Click Find Next or Find Prev until the record you want to delete is displayed in the text boxes, and then click Delete.

3. When the warning box appears, click OK to delete the record. (Keep in mind that you cannot undo a record deleted with the data form.) Click Close to return to the worksheet.

TIP To delete a record directly from the worksheet, right-click the row number containing the record you want to delete. Then select Delete from the shortcut menu to delete the row containing the record. If you use this method, be sure that you won't lose any data stored in the same row as the record you want to delete. If you want to undo the deletion, immediately choose Edit, Undo.

Databases: Finding Records

When you need to locate specific records in a database, you can use a *data form* to help you find them. You just enter the search criteria, and Excel finds the records corresponding to that criteria. (See "Databases: Creating a Database" before you complete this task.)

Steps

1. Select any cell in the database; then choose Data, Form.

2. Click the Criteria button; then type the criteria you want to search on in one or more text boxes. Excel performs the search only on the subset of data that matches the criteria you specify.

3. Click Find Next until you find the record you want; then click Close.

TIP If your database is small, you may prefer to use the data form to browse through the records in the database. Choose Data, Form; then click Find Next or Find Prev to find the desired record.

Databases: Inserting Records

A *data form* provides a convenient way to insert records in a database, as well as to search for and delete existing records. You also can insert records directly in the database by inserting rows in the worksheet. (See "Databases: Creating a Database" before you complete this task.)

Steps

1. Select any cell in the database; then choose Data, Form.

2. Click the New button; then type data for the new record in each of the text boxes.

3. Repeat Step 2 for each new record you want to add to the database.

4. Click Close when you are finished. The records you added are appended to the bottom of the database. You can sort the new records at any time if you want them to appear in a different order.

TIP   To erase the current entry in the data form as you are inserting new records, click the Restore button.

TIP   To insert a record directly in the worksheet, right-click the row number where you want the new row (record) to appear. Then select Insert from the shortcut menu to insert a blank row in the database.

(See also "Databases: Sorting a Database.")

Databases: Returning to the Original Sort Order

If you want to sort a database but later return it to the original order, you need to add a record index to the database. A record index can assign a number to each record according to the record's position or its date and time of entry. You may want to use a record index, for example, if you need to keep track of the order in which records are entered in a database. You can insert a column or cells to make room for an index.

(See "Databases: Creating a Database" and "Databases: Sorting a Database" in this section and "Inserting and Deleting: Columns" in the section "Editing Workbooks" before you complete this task.)

Steps

1. To index database records so that you can later return them to their original order, first insert a column for the index anywhere in the database. Many databases include an index field as the first column in a database. (If you named the database range, you need to redefine the name to include the new cells.)

2. Type a number, such as **1**, in the top cell of the column (beside the first database record). Type **2** in the second cell.

3. Select the cells containing 1 and 2 and drag the fill handle down the length of the database. When you release the mouse button, a series of numbers fill in next to each row. These are the index numbers.

NOTE   When you sort, always make sure that you include the column containing the index numbers. When you want to return the database records to their original order, select the column of index numbers in the Sort By list and select Ascending. ■

Databases: Sorting a Database

Excel enables you to organize the data in a database to suit your needs. Although sorting works best on databases, you can actually sort any data in your worksheet. You can sort data either alphabetically or numerically, in ascending or descending order. (See "Databases: Creating a Database" before you complete this task.)

Steps

1. Select any cell in the database; then choose Data, Sort.

2. In the Sort By box, select the field you want to sort on, then select either Ascending or Descending sort order.

3. If you want to sort on additional fields, select the fields in the Then By text boxes, and then select the sort order for each field. Click OK to perform the sort.

TIP To quickly sort the database on a single field, select any cell in that field. Then click either the Sort Ascending or Sort Descending button on the Standard toolbar.

NOTE Excel sorts date fields using the serial number created by dates and times entered in cells. Sorting works correctly only on dates and times entered with a date and time format that Excel recognizes. If you enter dates and times that Excel does not recognize, Excel normally stores them as text and sorts them in text order. (See also "Entering: Dates and Times" in the section "Editing Workbooks.") ■

(See also "Databases: Returning to the Original Sort Order.")

Forms: Adding Check Boxes

A check box is linked to a cell so that the result of the check box status appears as TRUE or FALSE in the linked cell. Selecting the check box makes the cell TRUE. Deselecting the check box makes the cell FALSE. The check box control is commonly used in a data form and provides an option to the user. (See "Forms: Adding Controls" before you complete this task.)

Steps

1. Draw a check box in the active worksheet by clicking the Check Box button on the Forms toolbar and then clicking the cell where you want the check box; then right-click the check box and choose Format Control from the shortcut menu.

2. Click the Control tab, then select the default value of the check box: Unchecked for FALSE result, Checked for TRUE result, or Mixed for #NA result. Choose the 3D Shading check box to add depth to the check box.

3. Select the Cell Link edit box, and click the cell that you want to hold the results of the check box; then click OK.

Forms: Adding Controls

Excel enables you to place on a worksheet the same type of data-entry controls that you can place in a dialog box run by a macro or Visual Basic procedure. *Controls* are data-entry objects commonly used in *forms*, such as scrolling lists or check boxes. When you enter a value in a control or make a selection from a control, the entry appears in a worksheet cell.

Steps

1. With a worksheet open, display the Forms toolbar by right-clicking in the toolbar area and choosing Forms.

2. Click the button on the Forms toolbar that represents the control you want to draw. To create a check box control, for example, click the Check Box button. The pointer changes to a crosshair.

3. Move the crosshair to the top-left corner of where you want the control to appear, and drag down and to the right to where you want the control's opposite corner.

4. Release the mouse button. The control appears in the worksheet. If you created a button control, the Assign Macro dialog box appears when you release the mouse button. Select the macro you want to assign to the control; then click OK.

5. To modify a control, hold down Ctrl and then click the control to select it. When a control is selected, handles appear around the object. You can then move, resize, or change the properties of the selected control. Drag an edge of the control to move it. Resize the control by dragging one of the handles.

 TIP To deselect a control, click a cell or object outside the selected control. To delete the control, select it and then press Delete.

TIP   Double-click a selected control to display the Format
Object dialog box. To change the format of the control, select the
options you want from the available tabs.

Forms: Adding Lists

Both a list box and a combo box restrict users to choosing
from a defined list of items. Restricting user selections prevents them from typing a mistake, entering incorrect data,
or using old data.

List boxes and combo boxes produce the same result, but the
appearance of the list in each type of box differs. A list box
shows multiple items in the list, while the list stays the same
height. A combo box is only one item high and has a drop-
down arrow on the right side. Clicking the drop-down arrow
displays the list. Combo boxes are commonly used when
not enough room exists for a list box. (See "Forms: Adding
Controls" and "Databases: Sorting a Database" before you
complete this task.)

Steps

1. In the worksheet, enter a vertical list of items you want
   to appear in the list. Enter one item per cell.

2. If you want the list to appear sorted within the control,
   select the list and choose Data, Sort to sort the list.
   Choose the desired sort options and then click OK.

3. Click the List Box or Combo Box button on the Forms
   toolbar and draw the control in the worksheet. Make a
   list box wide enough to see the entries in the list and tall
   enough to see multiple items. A combo box only needs to
   be tall enough for one item.

4. Right-click the list and choose Format Control; then click
   the Control tab.

5. Select the Input Range edit box; then drag across the
   range of cells in the worksheet that contain the data
   for the list. This list will appear in the list box or the
   combo box.

6. Select the Cell Link box and click the cell that will receive the results of the list. If you are using a combo box, enter in the Drop Down Lines box the number of lines displayed when the list appears; then click OK.

NOTE The cell you specify in the Cell Link box returns a value that represents the number of the selected list item, not the actual list item itself. However, you can use this number in a formula to return the selected item in the list. If a combo box is linked to cell B5 and the input range for the list is in the range C5:C10, for example, the following formula returns the value from range C5:C10 based on the selection from the combo box:

=INDEX(C5:C10,B5)

Forms: Adding Option Buttons

Option buttons are used most frequently when you need to make a single choice from a group of choices. Option buttons are round buttons that come in groups.

If you draw just option buttons on a worksheet, all these buttons will belong to the same group, which means that you can select only one button at a time. You can have multiple groups of buttons, however, by enclosing each group in a group box drawn with the group tool. (See "Forms: Adding Controls" before you complete this task.)

Steps

1. Draw a group box by clicking the Group Box button on the Forms toolbar and dragging where you want the box in the worksheet. While the box is selected, type a title to replace the default box title.

2. Click the Option Button tool on the Forms toolbar and draw an option button inside the group box. Type a title while the option button is selected.

3. Right-click the option button and choose Format Control; then click the Control tab. Select the value for the option button: Unchecked or Checked.

4. Select the Cell Link edit box, click the worksheet cell
   that you want to contain the results from the group of
   option buttons, and then click OK.

5. Repeat Steps 2 through 4 for each additional option
   button that you want to include. When you have
   finished creating option buttons, click a cell outside
   the group box.

NOTE When you create additional option buttons, you don't
have to enter a cell reference for the Cell Link. Only one linked
cell exists for all option buttons in a group. ■

Forms: Adding Scroll Bars

Scroll bars enable users to enter a number within a wide range
while getting a visual impression of where their entry lies
within the range. To enter a number, you can click the top or
bottom arrow, click the gray part of the scroll bar, or drag the
square button in the scroll bar. (See "Forms: Adding Controls"
before you complete this task.)

Steps

1. Draw a scroll bar control in the worksheet by clicking
   the Scroll Bar button on the Forms toolbar and dragging
   where you want the scroll bar; then right-click the
   control and choose Format Control from the shortcut
   menu.

2. Click the Control tab. In the Current Value edit box,
   enter the amount you want the linked cell to have when
   the worksheet opens.

3. Enter the lowest value you want the scroll bar to produce
   in the Minimum Value box. Enter the highest value you
   want in the Maximum Value box.

4. Set the amount of change for each click of the control in
   the Incremental Change box. In the Page Change edit
   box, enter the amount of change you want when the user
   clicks the gray part of the scroll bar.

5. Select the Cell Link edit box and then click the cell in the worksheet you want to receive the scroll bar result; then click OK.

Forms: Adding Spin Boxes

Spin boxes are controls that show two arrow heads—one pointing up and the other pointing down. Each click of an arrow head increases or decreases the amount in the cell linked to the spin box. Holding down the mouse button on a spin box causes the number to change continuously. (See "Forms: Adding Controls" before you complete this task.)

Steps

1. Draw a spin box in the worksheet by clicking the Spinner button on the Forms toolbar and dragging where you want the spin box; then right-click the spin box and choose Format Control from the shortcut menu.

2. Click the Control tab. In the Current Value edit box, enter the amount you want the linked cell to have when the worksheet opens.

3. Enter the lowest value you want the spin box to produce in the Minimum Value box. Enter the highest value you want in the Maximum Value box. Set the amount of change for each click of the control in the Incremental Change box.

4. Select the Cell Link edit box and then click the cell in the worksheet that you want to receive the spin box result; then click OK.

Forms: Creating a Form

Excel has many features that enable you to create nice-looking and easy-to-use data entry forms. Before you can create a data entry *form* using the Template Wizard, you need to create a worksheet that will be the basis for your form. Using Excel formatting techniques, you can make worksheets appear more like a paper form. You probably want to start by having the

DATA ANALYSIS

form in the same workbook as the worksheets that do the calculations, which makes it easier to create and maintain links from the controls on the form to the worksheets using the data. (See also "Template Wizard: Creating a Form" and "Forms: Adding Controls.")

Enhancing the Appearance of a Form

In most cases, you probably want the form you create to resemble a paper form rather than a typical worksheet. To do this, you can change several Window Options that appear on the View tab of the Options dialog box. The following table describes the recommended settings for these options when you are creating a form.

Recommended Window Options for Forms

Option	Description
Page Breaks	Deselect so automatic page breaks do not show.
Formulas	Deselect so results show, not formulas.
Gridlines	Deselect so gridlines do not show.
Row & Column Headers	Deselect so row and column headings are hidden.
Outline Symbols	Deselect unless your form is built in an outline.
Zero Values	(Optional) Deselect to hide zeros.
Horizontal Scroll Bar	Deselect to hide the scroll bar at the bottom.
Vertical Scroll Bar	Deselect to hide the scroll bar on the right edge.
Sheet Tabs	Deselect to hide the worksheet tabs.

Steps

1. To create a form and make the worksheet window look like a paper form, choose Tools, Options; then click the View tab.

2. Select from the options in the Window Options group to affect the appearance of only the active window. For recommendations on which options are most appropriate for forms, see the table above.

3. Enter the text labels you want to include in your form; enter these labels in cells above or to the left of the cells that will contain the data input.

4. To enhance the appearance of the form, format the workbook data as desired using the buttons on the Formatting toolbar, for example. You also can add controls to the form, such as check boxes.

5. Remember to print the form to check that the printed copy looks acceptable.

TIP Change the background color of a form to light gray to give it a more interesting appearance. Use the Shadow button on the Drawing toolbar to give pictures, charts, or text boxes a more three-dimensional appearance.

Forms: Formatting Controls

After you have drawn a control such as a check box on the worksheet, you can change the appearance of the control. You may want to change the font of the control, for example, so that it conforms with the fonts used in other worksheet data. (See "Forms: Adding Controls" and "Forms: Adding Check Boxes" before you complete this task.)

Steps

1. Right-click the control that you want to format, and then choose Format Control from the shortcut menu.

2. In the Format Control dialog box, click a tab, then select formatting options you want to apply to the control. Click OK when you have finished.

NOTE The Format Control dialog box used to format controls on forms may contain a different number and type of tab, depending on the control that you format. ■

Goal Seek

NOTE This feature's task requires understanding of a complex subject. If you are not familiar with the Goal Seek feature, you will probably want to become acquainted with it by reading *Special Edition Using Microsoft Excel 97* for a complete tutorial coverage. ■

Although *Goal Seek* is similar to the *Solver* add-in, it is generally faster and easier to use because it doesn't provide as many options as Solver does. Use Goal Seek if you want to produce a specific value in a formula cell by adjusting one input cell that influences a value; otherwise, if you have one or more input cells and have constraints on the solution, or if you want to maximize or minimize a formula cell, use Solver. (See also "Solver: Using Solver.")

You can use Goal Seek when you want to find an input value that generates the answer you want in a formula cell. To find the level of sales required to break even, for example, the formula cell would contain the net present value, and you would want the NPV function to return a zero value (which represents a break-even figure).

Steps

1. Select a goal cell that contains the formula you want to force to produce a specific value.

2. Choose Tools, Goal Seek. The Set Cell text box references the cell you selected in Step 1 above.

3. In the To Value text box, type the target value you want the formula cell to reach.

4. In the By Changing Cell text box, type the cell reference of the input cell (the cell you want to change); then click OK to start the goal seek process.

Outlines: Creating Manually

Outlining enables you to expand or contract worksheets or reports so that you see more or less detail. In a sales report, for example, you might need to display various levels of detail depending upon who will read the report. With the outline feature, you can hide or display up to eight levels of detail in rows or columns.

Excel can automatically create an outline, or you can manually create the outline. Manual outlining is necessary if the data is organized in a way that Excel doesn't understand. In general, you should arrange the worksheet so that summary rows are located below the detail rows, and summary columns are to the right of the detail columns. You may want to apply boldface or italic to summary rows or columns for emphasis, although this is not required for the outline feature to work. (See also "Outlines: Excel's Automatic Outlining" and "Outlines: Formatting Outlines.")

Steps

1. Select cells in the rows or columns that you want to outline. Select up to, but not including, the cell that contains the summary formula. If the rows or columns include only the data to outline, you can select the rows or columns to group.

2. To group items on a level, choose Data, Group and Outline, Group. The Group dialog box appears.

3. In the Group dialog box, select Rows or Columns, depending upon what you want to group; then click OK.

4. Repeat Steps 1 through 3 above for each section you want to outline.

NOTE If you selected an entire row or column in step 1, you don't see the Group dialog box. Excel groups the data by rows if you have rows selected or by columns if you have columns selected. ▪

TIP If you make a mistake or if you want to undo a grouping, you can use the Ungroup command. Select the section you want to ungroup. Then choose Data, Group and Outline, Ungroup. Select either Rows or Columns; then click OK.

Outlines: Displaying or Hiding Levels

You use the outline symbols to select which levels in an outline you want to display or hide. When you create an outline, the outline symbols appear automatically in a gray area to the left of the row numbers. (See "Outlines: Creating Manually" or "Outlines: Excel's Automatic Outlining" before you complete this task.)

Steps

1. If outline symbols are not displayed, press Ctrl+8. This key combination works as a toggle, to display or hide the outline symbols.

2. Display or hide levels of detail in specific rows or columns by following these actions, as desired:

   - Expand a specific row or column by clicking the related Display (+) symbol.

   - Expand to an entire level by clicking the appropriate Level number button. The Level number buttons appear at the top of the gray area that displays the outline symbols. To display all levels, click the highest numbered button.

   - Collapse a specific row or column by clicking the related Hide (-) symbol.

   - Collapse to a level by clicking the appropriate Level number button. To collapse all levels, click the lowest numbered button.

Outlines: Excel's Automatic Outlining

You can have Excel create an outline for you automatically instead of creating the outline manually. Automatic outlining is useful if you haven't created an outline before or your outline has a consistent layout. (See also "Outlines: Creating Manually.")

Steps

1. If you want to outline data within a part of the worksheet, select the range you want to outline. If you want to outline the entire worksheet, select a single cell.

2. Choose Data, Group and Outline, Auto Outline.

If Excel can determine a consistent direction of summarizing, it creates an outline. If Excel doesn't create an outline, it displays a warning message. If this occurs, you need to adjust the layout of your data or create an outline manually. (See "Outlines: Creating Manually.")

Outlines: Formatting Outlines

If you are creating a new outline, you can apply outline styles when Excel creates the outline. You also can apply outline styles to an existing outline. (See "Outlines: Creating Manually" or "Outlines: Excel's Automatic Outlining" before you complete this task.)

Steps

1. If you are formatting an existing outline, select the cells to which you want to apply the outline styles. Otherwise, begin with Step 2.

2. Choose Data, Group and Outline, Settings. The Settings dialog box appears.

3. If you are formatting an existing outline, choose Apply Styles. Otherwise, select Automatic Styles and then click OK.

Outlines: Hiding Symbols

You can choose whether or not you want to display the outline symbols in a worksheet that includes an outline. For example, if your worksheet is outlined, you may choose to hide the outline symbols while showing the worksheet during an on-screen presentation. (See "Outlines: Creating Manually" or "Outlines: Excel's Automatic Outlining" before you complete this task.)

Steps

1. To hide outline symbols in a worksheet, choose Tools, Options; then click the View tab.

2. Clear the Outline Symbols check box; then click OK.

TIP To toggle between hiding and showing outline symbols, add the Show Outline Symbols button to an existing toolbar. Choose Tools, Customize; then click the Commands tab. In the Categories list, select Data. Scroll through the Commands list until you see the Show Outline Symbols icon. Drag the icon to the desired location in an existing toolbar; then click Close. To remove the icon, choose Tools, Customize; then drag the icon off the toolbar and click Close.

Outlines: Removing an Outline

You can remove either a portion of an existing outline or the entire outline. (See "Outlines: Creating Manually" or "Outlines: Automatic Outlining" before you complete this task.)

Steps

1. To remove a portion of an outline, select cells in the row or columns at the level you want removed; or, to clear the entire outline, select a single cell in the worksheet.

2. Choose Data, Group and Outline, Clear Outline.

Pick from List: Building a List of Entries

Using Excel's AutoComplete feature, you can type the first few letters of an existing column entry, and Excel completes the rest of the entry for you. A similar feature, called Pick from List, enables you to select from a list of entries when you enter text in that column. Excel builds the list from entries that you have already made in the column above the active cell. You will save much time and repetitive typing with these two features. (See also "AutoComplete: Entering Duplicate Data.")

Steps

1. Select the cell in which you want to enter data.

2. To display a list of existing entries in the current column, right-click the cell; then choose Pick From List on the shortcut menu. A drop-down list appears.

3. Select an item from the list to complete the entry, or press Esc to close the list without choosing an entry.

 TIP Use Pick From List when you have many entries in a column where the first several characters are identical. In this case, picking from the list of entries is usually faster than typing the several characters required for autocompletion of your entry.

Pivot Tables: Adding a Data Field

In some cases, you may want to examine more than one kind of data in an existing *pivot table*. To do this, you use the PivotTable Wizard to add a second field to the DATA area. (See "Pivot Tables: Creating a Pivot Table" before you complete this task.)

Steps

1. To add another data field to an existing pivot table, select a cell in the pivot table.

2. Click the PivotTable Wizard button on the PivotTable toolbar. (Right-click the toolbar area and choose PivotTable to display this toolbar, if necessary.)

3. In Step 3 of the PivotTable Wizard, drag the button for the data field you want to add to the DATA area; then click Finish.

Pivot Tables: Adding Rows, Columns, or Pages

If you want to include more detail in an existing *pivot table*, you can add more fields to the display of a pivot table. To do this, you use the PivotTable Wizard. (See "Pivot Tables: Creating a Pivot Table" before you complete this task.)

Steps

1. To add a row, column, or page field to an existing pivot table, select a cell in the pivot table.

2. Click the PivotTable Wizard button on the PivotTable toolbar. (Right-click the toolbar area and choose PivotTable to display this toolbar, if necessary.)

3. In Step 3 of the PivotTable Wizard, drag the button for the desired field to the ROW, COLUMN, or PAGE area; then click Finish.

TIP   To remove a row, column, or page field from an existing pivot table, drag the field button outside of the pivot table.

Pivot Tables: Creating a Pivot Table

NOTE   This feature's task requires understanding of a complex subject. If you are not familiar with pivot tables, you will probably want to become acquainted with them by reading *Special Edition Using Microsoft Excel 97* for a complete tutorial coverage. ■

A *pivot table* enables you to summarize, analyze, and manipulate data in lists and tables. When you use the *PivotTable Wizard* to create a pivot table, you tell Excel which fields in the list you want to arrange in rows and columns. You also can specify a page field that appears to arrange the data in a stack of pages. Pivot tables are called such because you can quickly rearrange the position of pivot table fields to give you a different view of the table.

You can create a pivot table from several sources. The default (and most common) choice is to create a pivot table from an Excel list or database. In addition, you can create the pivot table from data in an external data source, multiple consolidation ranges, or another pivot table.

One useful application of pivot tables is creating summary tables that group large categories of data, with totals displayed for each category. After you create a pivot table, you can also more easily create charts based on data in the summarized table.

Steps

1. Select any cell in the list you want to summarize; then choose Data, PivotTable Report.

2. In Step 1 of the PivotTable Wizard, select the Microsoft Excel List or Database option (the source of the data); then click Next.

3. In Step 2 of the PivotTable Wizard, the range for the list appears in the Range text box. If this range is incorrect, type the correct range. Then, click Next.

4. In Step 3 of the PivotTable Wizard, you define the column and row layout of the pivot table. The fields are listed as buttons on the right side of the dialog box. Drag into the DATA area the button corresponding to the data field you want to summarize. To arrange items in a field in columns with the labels across the top, drag the button for that field to the COLUMN area. To arrange items in a field in rows with labels along the side, drag the button for that field to the ROW area. Then click Next.

5. In Step 4 of the PivotTable Wizard, specify where you want the pivot table to appear. (Be sure to choose an area that won't overwrite existing data.) If you want to specify additional options for the pivot table, click the Options button, choose the options you want, and click OK. Then, click Finish.

Pivot Tables: Editing a Pivot Table

Because *pivot tables* are devices for displaying information, you cannot manually change information in the body of the table.

You can, however, change the names of the pivot table fields and items. Excel doesn't allow you to duplicate names. If you enter an existing field or item name inadvertently, Excel rearranges the pivot table, moving the item with that name to the location where you typed the name. (See "Pivot Tables: Creating a Pivot Table" before you complete this task.)

Steps

1. To edit a pivot table field or item name, select that field or item in the pivot table.

2. Type the new name and press Enter.

 TIP To change additional options for a specific pivot table field, double-click the field button. Choose the options you want in the PivotTable Field dialog box; then click OK.

Pivot Tables: Formatting a Pivot Table

You can use the *AutoFormat* feature to apply a set of predefined formatting choices to a pivot table, just as you can for other tables in a worksheet. This will greatly enhance the appearance and readability of a pivot table. (See "Pivot Tables: Creating a Pivot Table" before you complete this task.)

Steps

1. With the pivot table you want to format active, choose Format, AutoFormat.

2. In the Table Format list, select the desired table format; then click OK.

(See also "Formatting: Tables with AutoFormats" in the "Formatting" section.)

Pivot Tables: Updating a Pivot Table

A *pivot table* does not change automatically when you change the data in the source list or table. You can, however, update or refresh the pivot table for the following types of changes to the source data: changes to data in a data field, new or changed items, or insertions or deletions of fields or items. (See "Pivot Tables: Creating a Pivot Table" before you complete this task.)

Steps

1. To update a pivot table, select any cell in the pivot table.
2. Click the Refresh Data button on the PivotTable toolbar.

Solver: Changing Solver Options

You can customize Solver options, such as how you want Solver to find answers, how long Solver works, or the precision of the answer it attempts to find. In most cases, however, the default settings should be appropriate for Solver problems. (See "Solver: Using Solver" before you complete this task.)

Steps

1. Open the workbook that contains the source data for Solver, and then choose Tools, Solver to display the Solver Parameters dialog box.

2. Click the Options button. The Solver Options dialog box appears.

3. Change the options, as desired. If you need more information on a particular option, click the question mark button, and then click the option for which you need help. Click OK when you've finished.

Solver: Installing Solver

Even if you installed the Solver option when you installed Excel, you still need to make the Solver add-in available by selecting it in the Add-Ins dialog box before you can begin to use it. After following this procedure, the Solver add-in will be available whenever you need to use the program.

Steps

1. From any point in Excel, choose Tools, Add-Ins.

2. In the Add-Ins Available list, select the Solver Add-In check box. If you don't see the Solver Add-In in the list, click Browse and then select the file named

SOLVER.XLA (check the \LIBRARY\SOLVER folder); then click OK.

3. Click OK again to close the Add-Ins dialog box.

NOTE If you can't locate the SOLVER.XLA file, you need to run the Setup program to install the file. ■

Solver: Producing Reports

Solver can generate reports summarizing the solution results. These reports enable you to easily compare different solutions to the same problem.

Solver can generate an Answer Report, a Sensitivity Report, and a Limits Report. The Answer Report summarizes the original and final values of the variables, target cell, and the constraints. The Sensitivity Report tells you how sensitive the solution is, based on small changes made to the target cell formula. The Limits Report shows how the solution changes when target and adjustable cells are maximized or minimized while other variables are held constant. (See "Solver: Using Solver" before you complete this task.)

Steps

1. After using Solver to solve a problem in the worksheet, the Solver Results dialog box appears; select one or more of the reports from the Reports list. Use Ctrl+click if you want to select multiple reports.

2. Click the Help button if you need more information on a particular report. Click OK when you are ready to generate the reports.

Each report you selected appears on its own worksheet. Select a sheet tab to browse through the reports and the original worksheet.

Solver: Saving and Loading Solver Data

Excel enables you to save and later reload different Solver settings and results by using the Save Model option in the

Solver Options dialog box. This allows you to easily switch between the various models you've created in a Solver problem. (See "Solver: Using Solver" before you complete this task.)

Steps

1. Open the workbook that contains the source data for Solver, and then choose Tools, Solver to display the Solver Parameters dialog box.

2. Click the Options button. The Solver Options dialog box appears.

3. Click the Save Model option. Then select a range of cells on the worksheet large enough to contain the number of constraints plus three additional cells.

4. Click OK to accept the range in the Save Model dialog box; click OK again when the Solver Options dialog box appears. Click Close to return to the worksheet.

5. To reload Solver models that you've already saved, click the Load Model button in the Solver Options dialog box. Specify the range for the model data you want to load, and click OK.

Solver: Using Solver

NOTE   This feature's task requires understanding of a complex subject. If you are not familiar with the Solver, you will probably want to become acquainted with it by reading *Special Edition Using Microsoft Excel 97* for a complete tutorial coverage. ∎

Unlike *Goal Seek*, which finds a specific solution to a problem, *Solver* finds an optimal solution by adjusting input cells while ensuring that other formulas in the worksheet stay within limits you specify. Use the Solver add-in to determine the maximum or minimum value of one cell by changing the adjustable cells—for example, the maximum profit to be generated by changing overhead expenditures. (See also "Goal Seek.")

Before you use Solver, include the following inputs in the worksheet: adjustable cells; the objective formula that you want to maximize or minimize; and the constraints, which place limits on the Solver problem.

NOTE   If Solver has not been installed, the Solver option doesn't appear in the Tools menu. If this is the case, see "Solver: Installing Solver" prior to doing the steps below. ■

Using the Solver Sample Worksheets

To make it easier for you to set up your own Solver problems in the worksheet, Excel comes with an on-line workbook that shows you specific examples of the types of problems you can use Solver to solve. Open the SOLVSAMP.XLS workbook (usually in the \EXAMPLES\SOLVER folder) to see these examples. If you don't see this workbook, you need to run the Excel Setup program to install it. After you open the workbook, switch to the worksheet containing the example you want to see, then choose Tools, Solver. The target cell, adjustable cells, and constraints for the worksheet are already specified.

Steps

1. Open the workbook that contains the source data for Solver, and then choose Tools, Solver; the Solver Parameters dialog box appears. In the Set Target Cells box, enter a cell reference or name for the target cell; the target cell must contain a formula.

2. For the value of the target cell to be as large as possible, click Max. For the value of the target cell to be as small as possible, click Min. For the value of the target cell to have a specified value, click Value of; then type the specific value in the box.

3. In the By Changing Cells box, enter a name or cell address for each adjustable cell, separating nonadjacent cell references with commas.

4. To have Solver automatically propose the adjustable cells based on the target cell, click Guess. In the Subject to the Constraints box, enter any constraints to be applied; then click Solve.

TIP If you want to restore the original values in the worksheet after you use Solver, click the Restore Original Values option in the Solver Results dialog box.

NOTE The selected cells must be related through formulas in the worksheet. Otherwise, changing one cell will not change the other. ■

Template Wizard: Creating a Form

With the *Template Wizard*, Excel enables you to create professional-looking data entry forms that make it easier for others to enter data into an Excel database. The Template Wizard guides you through the process of converting your worksheet into a data entry form. (See "Forms: Creating a Form" before you complete this task.)

Steps

1. To create a data entry form using the Template Wizard, open or create the workbook that contains the data you want to use for the form.

2. Choose Data, Template Wizard. If you don't see the Template Wizard option, you need to install this add-in before you can continue. Search on "Template Wizard" in Excel Help for more information.

3. Follow the steps in the Template Wizard.

4. Click Finish when you are done creating the template.

5. Save the worksheet that contains the template.

NOTE To enter data using the data entry form you have created, create a new workbook based on the template you created. The new workbook contains all the formatting, formulas, and data contained in the template, but it must be saved using a different name. ■

(See also "Templates: Creating and Using a Workbook Template" in the section "Customizing.")

Template Wizard: Using Excel's Templates

Excel provides several prebuilt templates for your use. Not all of these Excel templates are installed if you used the standard installation, however. To install additional templates, run the Setup program again, and choose the Custom installation option. (See also "Templates: Creating and Using a Workbook Template" in the section "Customizing.")

The Invoice, Expense Statement, and Purchase Order templates provided with Excel are designed for use with the Template Wizard.

Steps

1. With Excel open, choose File, New to use one of Excel's predefined templates.

2. Click the Spreadsheet Solutions tab; then click the icon representing the template you want to use. A preview of the template appears in the Preview box.

3. Click OK to open the selected template. Click the Customize button in the template if you want to customize the template. This enables you to insert your company logo, name, address, and so on.

4. Save the file using a different name when you've finished customizing the template.

 TIP   Use the custom toolbar provided with Excel's templates to perform actions on the template. Point to a button on the toolbar and pause to see a brief description of the button's purpose.

Editing Workbooks

After you have created a new *workbook* and entered data into it, you will eventually want to edit cell data or modify the structure of the workbook itself. You can edit the contents of a cell by retyping data into the cell or by editing the existing cell contents. To save time, you can copy and paste existing cell data rather than having to reenter the data. Excel also enables you to easily find and replace worksheet data, spell check your worksheet, and protect your data from unauthorized changes.

You can modify the structure of the workbook by adjusting column widths and row heights, and inserting or deleting cells, rows, columns, or worksheets. This section covers these features and more of the most-used means of editing your workbooks and worksheets.

Adjusting: Column Widths

You can improve the appearance of your *worksheet* by adjusting the width of columns to fit the data contained in those columns. Adjusting column widths can also help you fit more data on-screen or in a printout. If a column is not wide enough to display a number, date, or time, Excel displays #### characters in the cell. Excel also enables you to hide confidential data within a column. (See also "Alignment: Shrinking Text to Fit in a Cell" in the "Formatting" section.)

Steps

1. Move the pointer onto the right boundary of the column heading. To change the width of column B, for example, move the pointer onto the line between the B and C headers. The pointer changes to a two-headed, horizontal arrow.

2. Drag the column left or right until you reach the desired width; then release the mouse button.

To size multiple columns, select the columns, and then drag the right boundary of one of the selected columns. To size all columns in the worksheet, click the Select All button (the gray rectangle just left of the column letters), drag the right boundary of any column to the desired width, and then release the mouse button. (See "Selecting: Rows and Columns.")

TIP To automatically fit the column to its widest entry, double-click the right boundary of the column letter.

Adjusting: Row Heights

The height of a row automatically adjusts to the largest font size applied to a cell in a row unless you manually change the height of a row. Excel enables you to manually adjust the height of a row when you need additional space between rows of data. If you adjust the height of a row so that it is too small to display the font, the tops of the characters are cut off at the boundary of the cell(s) above.

Steps

1. Move the pointer onto the bottom boundary of the row heading. To change the height of row 7, for example, move the pointer onto the line between row numbers 7 and 8. The pointer changes to a two-headed, vertical arrow.

2. Drag the row up or down until you reach the desired row height; then release the mouse button.

To size multiple rows, select the rows, then drag the bottom boundary of one of the selected rows. To size all rows in the worksheet, click the Select All button (the gray rectangle just above the row numbers), drag the bottom boundary of any row to the desired height, and then release the mouse button. (See "Selecting: Rows and Columns.")

TIP To automatically make the row height fit the contents of the row, double-click the bottom boundary of the row number.

Copying: Cell Data

In Excel, you can copy cell data within a worksheet, between worksheets, between workbooks, or even between Excel and another application. (See also "Copying: Data Between Applications" and "Moving: Cell Data.")

Steps

 1. Highlight the cell or range you want to copy; then click the Copy button on the Standard toolbar (or choose Edit, Copy).

 2. Select the cell in the upper-left corner of the range where you want to copy the data; then click the Paste button on the Standard toolbar (or choose Edit, Paste).

 TIP To quickly copy data to another location in the same worksheet, highlight the cell or range you want to copy. Press and hold down the Ctrl key, and drag the border around the selected range to the desired location. Release the mouse button and the Ctrl key.

(See also "Pasting: Multiple Copies" in this section and "Copying Formats with the Format Painter" in the "Formatting" section.)

Copying: Data Between Applications

You can use the Clipboard to easily copy and paste data between Windows applications. The *Clipboard* is a temporary storage area for cut or copied items. When you cut or copy text or objects in one of the programs, Windows places that item on the Clipboard. You can then paste that item to the same worksheet, a different worksheet, or a different program.

EDITING WORKBOOKS

You can continue to paste the same item over and over again until you cut or copy another item.

Steps

1. Highlight the cell or range you want to copy; then click the Copy button on the Standard toolbar (or choose Edit, Copy).

2. Switch to the other application and select the location where you want to copy the data. If you are copying from Excel to Word, for example, switch to Word and position the insertion point where you want the copied data to appear.

3. Click the Paste button on the Standard toolbar (or choose Edit, Paste).

(See also "Pasting: Formats, Values, or Transposed Data" in this section and "Linking: Data Between Applications" in the "Linking and Embedding" section.)

Copying: Worksheets

You can copy all the contents and formatting of an existing worksheet to a new worksheet—either in the same workbook or to another workbook. This feature is useful if you frequently create similar worksheets, or if you need to start a new monthly or quarterly worksheet using the same format as an existing worksheet. (See also "Moving: Worksheets.")

Steps

1. Open the source and destination workbooks. Then display the source workbook (the workbook containing the worksheet you want to copy).

2. Right-click the tab of the worksheet that you want to copy; then choose Move or Copy from the shortcut menu.

3. In the To Book list, select the workbook to which you want to copy the selected worksheet.

4. In the Before Sheet list box, select which sheet you want the copied sheet placed in front of.

5. Select the Create a Copy check box to place a copy of the original worksheet in the selected workbook, while leaving the original worksheet intact; then click OK.

TIP To quickly create a copy of a worksheet in the same workbook, select the sheet tab for the worksheet you want to copy. Then press and hold down the Ctrl key and drag a copy of the active sheet tab forward or backward, to where you want the new worksheet to appear.

Deleting: Cell Contents

Although deleting data is a simple task, there are a few concepts with which you should become familiar. You can delete the data contained in worksheet cells, or you can delete the actual cells themselves. Deleting cell contents is sometimes referred to as clearing cell contents. When you clear cell contents, you have the option of clearing just the data in the cell, the cell formatting, cell comments, or all of these.

NOTE To delete cell contents (as described in this section), use the Edit, Clear command or the Delete key. If you want to delete actual cells or entire rows or columns (including all data contained in them), however, you would use the Edit, Delete command. (See "Inserting and Deleting: Cells and Ranges.")

Steps

1. Highlight the cell or range of data you want to clear.

2. Choose Edit, Clear; then select the option describing what you want to clear from the range: All, Formats, Contents, or Comments.

Choose Edit, Undo Clear to return the data range to its original state.

TIP To quickly clear just the contents from a range, select the range and then press Delete.

Deleting: Worksheets

If you no longer need a particular worksheet in a workbook, you can delete the entire worksheet. Excel prompts you for confirmation before deleting the worksheet. Exercise caution when using this command—if you delete a worksheet by accident, you cannot use Undo to restore the worksheet. (See also "Workbooks: Deleting a Workbook" in the "File Management" section.)

Steps

1. Right-click the sheet tab of the worksheet you want to delete.

2. Choose Delete; then click OK to confirm the deletion.

Editing Data: In a Cell

When you need to edit a cell entry, you can either edit the text in the cell itself or in the formula bar. For worksheets built like data-entry forms, the users often expect to type and edit directly in a cell.

Steps

1. Double-click the cell containing the text you want to edit. Move the I-beam pointer to where you want to edit, and click the mouse button.

2. Type the new data. If you want to delete text, use Backspace to delete text to the left of the insertion point or use Delete to remove text to the right of the insertion point.

3. Press Enter to accept your changes, or press Esc to leave the cell contents unchanged.

Editing Data: In the Formula Bar

In addition to editing data directly in the cell, you also can edit data from within the formula bar. If you frequently use the formula bar, you may prefer to edit data in the formula bar.

Steps

1. Select the cell containing the text you want to edit.

2. Move the pointer over the text in the formula bar until it changes to an I-beam. Move the I-beam pointer to where you want to edit the text, and then click the left mouse button.

3. Type the new data. If you want to delete text, use Backspace to delete text to the left of the insertion point or use Delete to remove text to the right of the insertion point.

4. Press Enter to accept your changes, or press Esc to leave the cell contents unchanged.

TIP To replace part of a cell entry, click and drag the I-beam pointer to highlight the characters you want to replace. Then, type the new data and press Enter.

Finding Worksheet Data

When your worksheets get large and are filled with data, you may have trouble finding specific information in them. The Find command enables you to jump to any piece of information, such as labels, formulas, values, or comments in your worksheet. (See also "Replacing Worksheet Data.")

Steps

1. Select the range you want to search; or to automatically search the entire worksheet, select a single cell only. (To begin the search from the beginning of the worksheet, select cell A1.)

2. Choose Edit, Find. In the Find What text box, type the data you want to find. Select any other search options you want in the Find dialog box (such as Match Case).

3. Click Find Next. Click Find Next again if you want to search for another occurrence. Click Close when you are finished.

NOTE   The Find command performs the search in the current worksheet only. To search in other worksheets in a workbook, you must select them individually, and then choose Edit, Find. ■

Grouping Worksheets

When you create a group of similar worksheets in a workbook (such as in a sales consolidation), you can group the worksheets together before you enter data or format the worksheets. This can save you a great deal of editing time because you can apply the same operations to the entire group of worksheets at once. (See "Selecting: Worksheets" in the "Getting Started" section before you complete this task.)

Steps

1. Select the worksheets you want to group together. Notice that the title bar now contains [Group].

2. Begin entering and formatting data in one of the selected worksheets. The text you enter and format in the current worksheet also appears in all other worksheets in the group.

3. To separate the group into individual sheets, hold down the Shift key and click the sheet tab for the current worksheet.

(See also "Formatting: Multiple Worksheets" in the "Formatting" section.)

Hiding: Columns and Rows

When you generate a worksheet for multiple users, you may not want to print all the information that you enter. You can hide columns temporarily so that they do not print or appear on-screen. In addition to hiding columns, you also can temporarily hide entire rows of data in the worksheet if you don't want them to print or appear on-screen. Hiding columns or rows doesn't affect the results of formulas that refer to hidden cells.

Steps

1. Right-click the column heading of the column you want to hide, or right-click the row heading of the row you want to hide.

2. From the shortcut menu, choose <u>H</u>ide.

 TIP   If you often hide and redisplay the same columns or rows in your worksheets, you should create a custom view using the <u>V</u>iew, Custom <u>V</u>iews command. This command enables you to assign a name to the current worksheet view. You can then use the <u>V</u>iew, Custom <u>V</u>iews command to select the name of the view you want to display.

(See also "Hiding: Displaying Hidden Columns and Rows.")

Hiding: Displaying Hidden Columns and Rows

If one or more column letters or row numbers appear to be missing in the worksheet frame, this is because the columns or rows have been hidden from view. You can easily redisplay hidden columns or rows if you need to see or edit data in them. (See "Hiding: Columns and Rows" before you complete this task.)

Steps

1. In the worksheet frame, drag across a range of columns that spans the hidden column, or drag across a range of rows that spans the hidden row.

2. Right-click one of the selected columns or rows. From the shortcut menu, choose <u>U</u>nhide.

Inserting and Deleting: Cells and Ranges

You can insert new blank cells or delete existing cells anywhere in the worksheet. When you insert cells, the existing cells move in the direction you specify to make room for the new cells.

EDITING WORKBOOKS

When you delete cells from a worksheet, you delete the contents of the cells and the actual cells themselves. The remaining cells shift to fill the space left by the deleted cells. When you insert or delete cells or ranges, formulas that reference affected cells automatically update. (See also "Deleting: Cell Contents.")

Steps

1. Highlight the cell or range where you want to insert or delete a cell or range.

2. Choose Insert, Cells if you want to insert a cell or range; or choose Edit, Delete if you want to delete a cell or range.

3. Select which direction to move existing (or remaining) cells in the worksheet; then click OK.

Inserting and Deleting: Columns

As you edit your worksheet, you may need to insert or delete entire columns in the worksheet. Perhaps you forgot to add a category, and you now want to insert it between existing columns of data. Or you might want to delete a column containing outdated information. (See also "Inserting and Deleting: Rows.")

Steps

1. If you are inserting a column, select the column header of the column you want to move to the right when you insert the new column; or, if you are deleting a column, select the column header of the column you want to delete.

2. To insert a column, choose Insert, Columns; or, to delete the selected column, choose Edit, Delete.

TIP If you want to insert or delete multiple columns, select the same number of columns as you want to insert or delete in Step 1 above.

Inserting and Deleting: Rows

Just as you can insert or delete columns in the worksheet, you also can insert blank rows or delete existing rows. In a list of information, you can insert a row if you want to add a new record of data, for example, or you can delete a row if you no longer want to include a specific record in the list. (See also "Inserting and Deleting: Columns.")

Steps

1. If you are inserting a row, select the row header of the row you want to move down when you insert the new row; or, if you are deleting a row, select the row header of the row you want to delete.

2. To insert a row, choose Insert, Rows; or, to delete the selected row, choose Edit, Delete.

 TIP If you want to insert or delete multiple rows, select the same number of rows as you want to insert or delete in Step 1 above.

Inserting Worksheets

Each new workbook contains three worksheets by default. You can easily insert new worksheets (as many as 255 total) at any time. If you are copying or moving existing worksheets, you do not need to insert a blank worksheet before you copy or move a worksheet. (See also "Copying: Worksheets" and "Moving: Worksheets.")

Steps

1. Open the workbook to which you want to add a new worksheet.

2. Choose Insert, Worksheet. The new worksheet is inserted just before the current worksheet.

3. Drag the sheet tab of the new worksheet to where you want the worksheet to appear.

TIP You can change the default number of worksheets that appears in a new workbook. Choose Tools, Options; then click the General tab. In the Sheets in New Workbook text box, type the number of worksheets you want new workbooks to contain; then click OK.

Moving: Between Worksheets

The sheet tabs at the bottom of each workbook enable you to quickly move among the worksheets in that workbook. If your workbook contains multiple worksheets and some of the sheet tabs are hidden, you can increase the width of the sheet tab area by dragging the tab split box (the vertical bar just left of the horizontal scroll bar) to the right. If you still cannot see all the sheet tabs, use the tab scroll arrows to the left of the sheet tabs to move through the sheet tabs. With a single click, the tab scroll arrows enable you to move to either the first sheet, previous sheet, next sheet, or last sheet in the workbook.

Steps

1. Display the sheet tab for the worksheet to which you want to move.

2. Click the sheet tab to move to that worksheet.

NOTE If your workbook doesn't display any sheet tabs, choose Tools, Options; then click the View tab and select the Sheet Tabs check box. ■

Moving: Cell Data

In Excel, you can move cell data within a worksheet, between worksheets, between workbooks, or even between Excel and another application. When you move (or cut) cell data, you also move the cell formatting with the data. Be sure you won't overwrite any existing data when you move the data (make room for the data first, if necessary). (See also "Copying: Cell Data.")

Steps

 1. Highlight the cell or range you want to move; then click the Cut button on the Standard toolbar (or choose <u>E</u>dit, Cu<u>t</u>).

2. Select the cell in the upper-left corner of the range where you want to move the data. If you are moving the data to another application, switch to that application and navigate to where you want to place the data.

 3. Click the Paste button on the Standard toolbar (or choose <u>E</u>dit, <u>P</u>aste).

 TIP To quickly move data to another location in the same worksheet, highlight the cell or range you want to move. Drag the border around the selected range to the desired location.

Moving: Worksheets

You can move worksheets to a different location within the same workbook, or to another workbook entirely. You do not need to create a blank worksheet to receive the new data—you can move the worksheet directly to the new location. (See also "Copying: Worksheets.")

Steps

1. Open the source and destination workbooks. Then display the source workbook (the workbook containing the worksheet you want to move).

2. Right-click the tab of the worksheet that you want to move; then choose <u>M</u>ove or Copy from the shortcut menu.

3. In the <u>T</u>o Book list, select the workbook to which you want to move the selected worksheet.

4. In the <u>B</u>efore Sheet list box, select which sheet you want the moved sheet placed in front of; then click OK.

TIP To quickly move a worksheet in the same workbook, select the sheet tab for the worksheet you want to move. Then drag the active sheet tab in front of the sheet tab where you want the worksheet to appear.

NOTE To place a worksheet as the beginning worksheet in a new workbook without first creating the workbook, select (new book) in the To Book list in the Move or Copy dialog box. ▇

Naming Worksheets

Each worksheet in a workbook is automatically assigned a name. In a new workbook, worksheets are named Sheet1, Sheet2, and so on, as displayed on the sheet tabs. You can also assign your own descriptive name of up to 31 characters to each worksheet. You can use spaces in a worksheet name, but you cannot use any of the following characters:

/ \ : ? * [ ] < >

Steps

1. Double-click the sheet tab for the worksheet you want to rename.

2. Type the new name for the worksheet and press Enter.

Pasting: Formats, Values, or Transposed Data

With the Edit, Paste Special command, you can copy and paste part of a cell's attributes, such as the format or value, but not both. This command also enables you to transpose data by switching rows of cells to columns, and columns to rows. In addition, you can use this command to combine the attributes of cells by pasting them together.

Steps

1. Select the cell or range of cells you want to paste, and then click the Copy button on the Standard toolbar.

2. Select the cell in the upper-left corner of where you want to paste the data. Be sure to select an area where you

won't overwrite existing cell data. Then, choose <u>E</u>dit,
Paste <u>S</u>pecial.

3. In the Paste area, select the characteristics you want
   transferred: <u>A</u>ll, <u>F</u>ormulas, <u>V</u>alues, Forma<u>t</u>s, <u>C</u>omments,
   Validatio<u>n</u>, or All E<u>x</u>cept Borders.

4. In the Operation area, select how you want the transferred data combined with the cells you are pasting into:
   N<u>o</u>ne, A<u>d</u>d, <u>S</u>ubtract, <u>M</u>ultiply, or D<u>i</u>vide.

5. Select the Skip <u>B</u>lanks check box if you do not want to
   paste blank cells on top of existing cell contents. Select
   the Transpos<u>e</u> check box to change rows to columns or
   to change columns to rows; then click OK.

TIP   To quickly copy only the cell formats, select the cells with
the formats that you want to copy. Click the Format Painter button
on the Standard toolbar. Then select the range to copy the
formats to.

Pasting: Multiple Copies

You can save a great deal of data-entry time with Excel's Copy
and Paste commands and other shortcuts. Rather than typing
each formula in a worksheet, you can type a few formulas and
copy or fill them into other cells. You even can copy the formula and format at the same time. Be sure you won't overwrite
any existing data when you paste the copied data (make room
for the data first, if necessary).

Steps

1. Select the cell or range of cells you want to copy; then
   click the Copy button on the Standard toolbar.

2. Click and drag to select only the cells in the upper-left
   corner of where you want each of the duplicate ranges
   to go.

3. Click the Paste button on the Standard toolbar.

(See also "Copying: Cell Data" and "Moving: Cell Data.")

Pasting: Nonadjacent Multiple Copies

You can paste multiple copies of data even if the areas into which you are pasting are not adjacent. Be sure you won't overwrite any existing data when you paste the copied data (make room for the data first, if necessary). (See also "Pasting: Multiple Copies.")

Steps

1. Select the cell or range of cells you want to copy; then click the Copy button on the Standard toolbar.

2. Click the cells in the upper-left corner of each range where you want to paste the data. Hold down the Ctrl key as you click each cell.

3. Click the Paste button on the Standard toolbar.

Protecting: Cell Data

If you need to share worksheets with other users, you can prevent the contents of specific cells from being changed by turning on worksheet protection. You first must unlock cells that you want others to be able to change, and then protect the entire worksheet. (See also "Protecting: Individual Worksheets" and "Protecting: Workbooks.")

Steps

1. Select the range of cells you want to unlock. These are the cells that you do want others to be able to modify.

2. Choose Format, Cells; then click the Protection tab.

3. Clear the Locked check box so that it is not selected; then click OK.

4. Choose Tools, Protection, Protect Sheet.

5. Select the desired options describing what you want to protect in the current worksheet; then click OK.

NOTE You can assign a password so that only users with access to the password can make changes to the unlocked cells. In the Protect Sheet dialog box, type the password you want to use in the Password text box; then click OK. In the Confirm Password dialog box, reenter the same password and then click OK. ▪

To turn off worksheet (and therefore cell data) protection, choose Tools, Protection, Unprotect Sheet.

Protecting: Individual Worksheets

You can protect individual worksheets in a workbook if you want to prevent others from accessing them. Protecting a worksheet does not prevent others from opening the workbook and modifying other unprotected worksheets in the workbook, however. (If you want to protect an entire workbook, see "Protecting: Workbooks.")

Steps

1. Display the worksheet you want to protect; then choose Tools, Protection, Protect Sheet.

2. Select the desired options describing what you want to protect in the current worksheet.

3. If desired, type a password in the Password text box (passwords are case sensitive); then click OK.

4. If prompted, reenter the password in the confirmation box; then click OK.

To turn off worksheet protection, display the worksheet and choose Tools, Protection, Unprotect Sheet. Then, enter the password and click OK.

CAUTION Don't forget your password! When you protect a worksheet, write down the password and keep it in a safe location. You won't be able to open the worksheet or access any data in the worksheet without the password.

EDITING WORKBOOKS

Protecting: Opening a Protected Workbook

You can open a password-protected workbook just as you would normally open a workbook. Before the workbook appears on-screen, however, Excel prompts you for the password(s) you assigned to the workbook. If you do not remember the password for opening the workbook, you will not be able to access the workbook. If you forget only the password you set for write-protecting the workbook, you can open the workbook but you can't enter new data, even if you save the workbook under a different name. (See "Protecting: Workbooks" before you complete this task.)

Steps

1. Click the Open button on the Standard toolbar and select the workbook you want to open; then click Open.

2. In the Password dialog box, type the password and then click OK. Remember that passwords are case sensitive.

3. If a second Password dialog box appears, type the password for write (modify) access and then click OK; or click Read Only if you only want to view the workbook.

Protecting: Workbooks

You can prevent other users from accessing or changing the contents of a workbook by assigning password protection to a file. Excel provides three levels of protection: you can assign a workbook as read-only recommended, as write-protected, and as password-protected. The first setting suggests to users that they open a file in read-only mode. The last two options enable you to enforce protection by restricting file modification or access only to those who have the password.

Steps

1. Open the workbook you want to protect; then choose File, Save As, and click the Options button.

2. In the Save Options dialog box, enter the passwords you want to set—you can set one to open the workbook and

another to modify the workbook. Passwords are case sensitive.

3. Reenter the password(s) in the confirmation box(es); then click OK.

4. Select Read-Only Recommended if you want to recommend that others open a workbook as read-only (they must save the workbook with a different name if they want to save their changes—they cannot make any changes to the existing workbook); then click OK.

5. Click the Save button to save the workbook with your changes.

NOTE The Read-Only Recommended option doesn't override the password settings. If you assign a password to a workbook, only those who have access to the password can open the workbook and view the worksheet data.

To remove protection from a workbook, open the workbook and choose File, Save As; then click Options, remove the passwords from the Save Options dialog box (and clear the Read-Only Recommended check box, if applicable), and click OK. Then click Save to save the workbook with these changes.

CAUTION Don't forget your password. When you protect a workbook, write down the password and keep it in a safe location. You won't be able to open the workbook or access any data in the workbook without the password.

Replacing Worksheet Data

You can use the Replace command to quickly locate and replace one string of data with another. You can choose to replace all occurrences of a selected string, or you can replace a string one by one. (See also "Finding Worksheet Data.")

EDITING WORKBOOKS

Steps

1. Select the range you want to search; or to automatically search the entire worksheet, select a single cell only. (To begin the search from the beginning of the worksheet, select cell A1.)

2. Choose Edit, Replace. In the Find What text box, type the data you want to find. In the Replace With text box, enter the data to replace with; then click Find Next.

3. Click Replace to replace the first occurrence, and then click Find Next again if you want to search for another occurrence; or, click Replace All to replace all occurrences. Click Close when you are finished.

NOTE The Replace command performs the search in the current worksheet only. To search in other worksheets in a workbook, you must select them individually, and then choose Edit, Replace. ▨

Spelling: Creating Custom Dictionaries

You may need a custom dictionary with your worksheets so that you are not frequently prompted to verify the spelling of client names, abbreviations, product codes, industry terms, and so on. When Excel checks spelling, it looks first in the standard dictionary. If Excel doesn't find the word there, it checks the custom dictionary.

Unless you specify otherwise, words you add go into the dictionary named CUSTOM.DIC. This name appears in the Add Words To drop-down list in the Spelling dialog box. You can build your own custom dictionaries and select them from the list. You can have as many custom dictionaries as you like, but only one can operate at a time with the standard dictionary.

Steps

1. Open the worksheet containing words you want to add to a custom dictionary; then click the Spelling button on the Standard toolbar.

2. When the spell checker finds a word that you want in the custom dictionary, type the new dictionary name in the Add Words To text box.

3. Click Add to add the current word to the new dictionary.

At any time when the Spelling dialog box is open, you can change to a different custom dictionary by selecting the dictionary from the Add Words To list.

To add words to your custom dictionary, start the spell check. When you want to add a word to a custom dictionary, select the dictionary from the Add Words To list and choose the Add button.

Spelling: Running a Spell Check

With Excel's dictionary, you can check the spelling of one word, the entire worksheet, or even a chart. Microsoft Office applications all use the same spelling checker and dictionaries.

You also can check against a custom dictionary that contains abbreviations or words specific to your clients or industry.

Spelling Options

The following table lists the options available in the Spelling dialog box and describes how they work:

Options in the Spelling Dialog Box

Option	Description
Ignore	Ignores this word and continues.
Ignore All	Ignores this word throughout the document.
Add	Adds this word to the current dictionary.
Suggest	Suggests some alternatives from the dictionary. This option is available only if the Always Suggest check box is not selected; otherwise, Excel automatically provides suggested alternatives.
AutoCorrect	Adds this misspelling and the correction to the list of AutoCorrect entries. When you

continues

EDITING WORKBOOKS

Option	Description
	make this same mistake again, Excel automatically replaces the misspelling with the correct spelling.
Undo Last	Undoes the most recent spell check correction.
Cancel	Stops the spell check.

Steps

1. Select a single cell if you want to spell check the entire contents of a worksheet; or, select a range, embedded chart, or object to limit the spell check to the selected item. (To begin the spell check from the beginning of the worksheet, select cell A1.)

2. Click the Spelling button on the Standard toolbar. If a word cannot be found in the dictionary, the Spelling dialog box appears.

3. Accept or edit the word in the Change To text box; and then choose the Change button. Or, choose the Change All button if you want to change this word throughout the document.

   Alternatively, select one of the words from the Suggestions list, and then choose the Change or Change All button. You can also choose from the options in the table that precedes this task.

4. If prompted, choose Yes to continue from the top of the document.

5. When an alert box tells you that the entire worksheet has been checked, click OK.

NOTE If no misspelled words are found, the Spelling dialog box never appears. Instead, a message box appears and tells you that the spell check is complete for the entire worksheet. ■

File Management

This section shows you how to work with files, or *workbooks*, in Excel. The File menu provides several commands that perform basic file management tasks, such as saving files, opening existing files, creating new files, and closing files. In addition, you can use Excel to search for a file, add summary information to a workbook, and change the default folder used to open and save files.

If you work with others on a network, you can use the shared workbooks feature so that multiple users can view and modify a workbook simultaneously. You learn how to set up a shared workbook, view a history of changes made to the workbook, and discontinue sharing the workbook.

You can now use Excel to create hyperlinks to other Office documents as well as to Internet or intranet sites that you specify. The Web toolbar in Excel enables you to browse the Web and quickly navigate among favorite sites as well as Office documents.

Files: Changing the Default Folder

You can change the default folder used in Excel so that when you open an existing workbook or save a new workbook, the folder you choose automatically appears as the current folder. You can change the default folder to the folder where you most often store your workbook files.

Steps

1. With Excel open, choose Tools, Options; then click the General tab.

2. In the Default File Location text box, type the full path name (including the drive letter) for the folder you want to use as the default; then click OK.

Files: Displaying Quick View Information

You can use the Open dialog box in Excel to preview a workbook before you open the workbook. When you are deciding which file you want to open, copy, print, or delete, it is helpful to see a file's contents quickly, without having to open the file first. This feature, provided with Windows 95, is also available in Windows Explorer and other Windows applications.

Steps

1. With Excel open, choose File, Open to display the Open dialog box.

2. In the Look In drop-down list, select the drive and folder containing the workbook file you want to view.

3. In the list box, select the workbook.

4. Right-click the file name; then select Quick View from the shortcut menu. Excel displays the workbook in the Quick View window. You can use the scroll bars (or Page Up and Page Down) to scroll the window.

5. Click the Close button in the Quick View window to close the window; or, if you want to open the file, click the Open File for Editing button in the Quick View window.

NOTE   If you don't see the Quick View option in the shortcut menu, run the Windows 95 Setup program to install Quick View. ▩

Files: Searching for Files

When you want to work on a specific workbook, but can't remember exactly where you have stored it on disk or what you have named the file, you can use the Find File feature to help you track down the file.

Steps

1. With Excel open, choose File, Open; then click the Advanced button.

2. In the Property drop-down list, select the file property you want to search. In the Condition drop-down list, select the condition. In the Value text box, type the search value. To find all file names that start with "Sales", for example, choose File Name in the Property list, then choose Begins With in the Condition list, and type **Sales** in the Value text box.

3. In the Look In drop-down list, type the drive letter and folder name where you want to begin the search. If you want to also search subfolders, select the Search Subfolders check box.

4. Click the Add to List button. If desired, define additional criteria to narrow your search by repeating Steps 2 and 3 above.

5. To begin the search, click the Find Now button. All files meeting the specified criteria will appear in the list box of the Open dialog box. Double-click the file you want to open, or click Cancel to return to the worksheet.

TIP   If you want to save the information you use to perform a search, click the Save Search button in the Advanced Find dialog box; then type a name for the search and click OK. To later reopen the search, click the Open Search button in the Advanced Find dialog box; then select the name for the search and click OK.

Internet: Browsing Web Pages

If you work primarily within Excel, have access to the Internet, and occasionally need to jump to a Web page on the Internet, you will probably want to use Excel's Web toolbar to navigate between documents and the Internet Explorer (rather than working on documents from within Internet Explorer).

FILE MANAGEMENT

The buttons on the Web toolbar enable you to navigate forward or backward through *hyperlinks* in Web pages or Office documents. You can add references to favorite Web pages or Office documents to the Favorites button so that you can jump to them more quickly. You also can type a path or URL in the Address box on the Web toolbar to jump directly to that reference.

Steps

1. To start the Web browser from Excel (or another Office document), click the Web Toolbar button on the Standard toolbar (or choose <u>V</u>iew, <u>T</u>oolbars, Web).

2. Use one of the following methods to retrieve a document or Web page:

- Click the Start Page button to open the start page.
- Click the Search the Web button to open the Web search page.
- Type the URL in the Address box and press Enter.
- Select a previous URL from the Address list and press Enter.

- Click the Favorites button and select from the favorites list.

(See also "Publishing to the Web" in the "Producing Output" section.)

Internet: Creating Hyperlinks

In an Excel workbook, you can insert *hyperlinks* that enable you to quickly jump to Internet or intranet sites, or to other Excel workbooks or Office documents. When combined with a Web browser such as Internet Explorer, hyperlinks make it easy for the reader of a document to click a phrase or graphic in a workbook and immediately jump to a related Web page or document. This method is similar to the Excel on-line Help system—when you see a gray button with a double arrow on a Help screen, you click the button to jump to a page containing related information.

Steps

1. Select the cell that is to contain the hyperlink; then click the Insert Hyperlink button on the Standard toolbar (or choose Insert, Hyperlink).

2. In the Link to File or URL box, type the path or URL address that you want to link to. (Click the down arrow beside this box to see the proper format for typing URL addresses.)

3. If you want to jump to a specific location in a workbook or other document, type the location information (such as a range name in Excel or a bookmark name in Word) in the Named Location in File text box.

4. Select the Use Relative Path for Hyperlink check box if you want to be able to move all the linked files and their directories to a new location.

5. Click OK to insert the hyperlink in the workbook. The hyperlink appears in colored, underlined text.

To use the hyperlink you added to a workbook, connect to your Internet service provider (if the hyperlink is a link to an Internet site), and then click the cell containing the hyperlink.

To stop the jump before it is completed, click the Stop Current Jump button on the Web toolbar.

To return to the workbook containing the hyperlink after you view the linked document, click the Back button on the Web toolbar.

TIP To enter your own text in place of a hyperlink reference, right-click the cell containing the hyperlink; then choose Hyperlink, Select Hyperlink. Type a descriptive name for the hyperlink and then press Enter. You can point to the hyperlink to see the reference information for the link.

(See also "Publishing to the Web" in the "Producing Output" section.)

FILE MANAGEMENT

Opening: Existing Workbooks

To work on an existing workbook that has already been saved to disk, you must open the workbook file. Opening a workbook can be accomplished with a couple of mouse clicks. (See also "Workbooks: Creating a New Workbook.")

Steps

1. With Excel open, click the Open button on the Standard toolbar (or choose File, Open).

2. In the Look In drop-down list, select the drive and folder containing the workbook file you want to open.

3. In the list box, select the desired workbook; then click Open.

 TIP To open a recently used workbook, choose File. Then click the appropriate workbook name near the bottom of the File menu (just above the Exit command). By default, Excel displays up to four recently used files in the File menu. To change the default number of files displayed, choose Tools, Options; then click the General tab. In the Recently Used File List box, type the number of entries you want to display (between 1 and 9); then click OK.

 TIP To quickly open an Excel workbook from within Microsoft Explorer, double-click the workbook file name. This also opens the Excel program (if it wasn't already open).

(See also "Opening: Files Saved in Other File Formats.")

Opening: Files Saved in Other File Formats

The easiest way to import data from a non-Excel format into Excel is to import the data directly by using the Open dialog box. Excel can read many different file formats, such as Lotus 1-2-3, Quattro Pro, dBASE, and even HTML. In most cases, you will want to resave the data in Excel format after you open the file.

If you need to view only selected portions of data from a dBASE, Access, or Paradox file, or from another file arranged in row and column format, you may want to use Microsoft Query. Using Microsoft Query (an Excel add-in program), you can selectively extract information from a large file on disk without importing the entire file. For more information, search on "Microsoft Query" in the Excel on-line Help system.

Steps

 1. With Excel open, click the Open button on the Standard toolbar (or choose File, Open).

2. In the Files of Type drop-down list, select the type of file you want to open.

3. In the Look In drop-down list, select the drive and folder containing the file you want to open.

4. In the list box, select the desired file; then click Open.

CAUTION   Saving a file to a non-Excel format can result in the loss of formulas, functions, special features, and formatting that are unique to Excel 97. To save the original non-Excel file in Excel workbook format, be sure to choose Microsoft Excel Workbook in the Save as Type drop-down list box when you choose File, Save.

(See also "Saving: Workbooks as Different File Formats" in this section and "Importing Graphics" in the section "Charts and Graphics.")

Saving: Automatically Saving Workbooks

Excel includes the capability to save your workbooks for you, as you are working on them. With the AutoSave add-in, you can save your work automatically or have Excel prompt you to save your work. You determine how often to save and whether the setting is for the active workbook or all open workbooks.

FILE MANAGEMENT

1. With Excel open, choose Tools, AutoSave. If AutoSave doesn't appear on the Tools menu, choose Tools, Add-Ins; select the AutoSave check box in the Add-Ins available list box, and then click OK.

2. In the AutoSave dialog box, ensure that the Automatic Save Every check box is selected and enter the time interval for saving in the Minutes text box.

3. To AutoSave all open workbooks, select the Save All Open Workbooks option. Otherwise, select the Save Active Workbook Only option.

4. If you want to be prompted to save the workbook, ensure that the Prompt Before Saving check box is selected; then click OK.

(See also "Saving: Workbooks.")

Saving: Creating Automatic Backups

Excel can create a backup copy of your workbook every time you save the workbook. When you choose this option, Excel saves two copies of the file—one uses the file name you enter, and the other is named "Backup of *file name*." If the original workbook is lost or damaged, you can use the backup copy so that you can at least recover all the work you did up until you last saved the file. You must save a file more than once before a backup file is created. Excel stores the backup file in the same folder as the original workbook.

Steps

1. Display the workbook you want to save with an automatic backup; then choose File, Save As; then click the Options button. The Save Options dialog box appears.

2. Select the Always Create Backup check box; then click OK.

3. Click Save to save the active workbook.

(See also "Saving: Automatically Saving Workbooks.")

Saving: Workbooks

After you've created a workbook, you must save the workbook to permanently store the data on disk. The first time you save a file, you are prompted to specify the file name and the location on disk in which to store the file. After you have saved a file, each additional time you save the file, the existing version on disk is replaced with the new version. If you want to keep multiple versions of a workbook (if you think you may need to revert back to an earlier version), you should save the file using a different file name.

File names in Excel 97 can now use up to 255 characters, including spaces. Excel automatically appends the XLS extension to a file name when you save a workbook (depending on your Windows settings, you may not see this extension on-screen). You cannot use any of the following characters in a file name:

? : \ * , " | < >

NOTE   If you save a workbook using a name with more than eight characters (not including the file extension), the file name will automatically convert to an eight-character file name when transferred to earlier versions of Windows. The first portion of the name is shortened to six letters followed by a tilde (~), then a number (beginning with 1). For example, a workbook named INVOICEJUNE.XLS would shorten to INVOIC~1.XLS. The number at the end of the file name distinguishes names that might conflict with each other when they are renamed. In this example, the file name INVOICEJULY.XLS would be shortened to INVOIC~2.XLS. ■

Steps

 1. Display the workbook you want to save; then click the Save button on the Standard toolbar (or choose File, Save). If this is the first time you've saved the workbook, the Save As dialog box appears.

If you previously saved the workbook, Excel replaces the file on disk with the current version of the workbook, using the same file name—no dialog box displays.

FILE MANAGEMENT

2. In the Save In drop-down list, select the drive and folder where you want to save the file. In the File Name box, type the file name you want to use to save the file; then click Save.

NOTE   To save the current workbook with a different name, choose File, Save As. In the Save As dialog box, select a folder in the Save In drop-down list, type the new name in the File Name box, and then click Save. ■

TROUBLESHOOTING   **After saving a workbook in Excel 97, I can't open the file in an earlier version of Excel.** Because Excel 97 includes features not supported in earlier versions of Excel, you must resave the file in Excel 97 using a different file format. To save a workbook for use only in Excel 5.0 or Excel 95, for example, select Microsoft Excel 5.0/95 Workbook from the Save as Type list in the Save As dialog box. If you need to use the workbook in both Excel 97 and either Excel 5.0 or Excel 95, you should save your workbook by selecting Microsoft Excel 97 & 5.0/95 Workbook from the Save as Type list.

(See also "Saving: Automatically Saving Workbooks" and "Saving: Workbooks as Different File Formats")

Saving: Workbooks as Different File Formats

You can use the Save As dialog box to save an Excel workbook as a different file format, such as Lotus 1-2-3. This enables you to easily transfer work created in Excel to another program. If your Excel workbook includes features or formatting not supported by the other program, however, you may lose data or formatting when you use the file in the other program. (See "Saving: Workbooks" before you complete this task.)

Steps

1. Display the workbook you want to save as a different file format; then choose File, Save As.

2. In the Save as Type drop-down list, select the file type you want to use to save the workbook.

3. In the Save In drop-down list, select the drive and folder where you want to save the file.

4. In the File Name box, type the file name you want to use to save the file; then click Save.

NOTE If you work with others who use earlier versions of Excel or another spreadsheet program, you can set up Excel to use another format as the default for saving workbooks. Choose Tools, Options; then click the Transition tab. In the Save Excel Files As drop-down list, select the file format you want to use; then click OK. You can override this setting at any time in the Save As dialog box. Keep in mind that if you change the default to an earlier version of Excel, you won't be able to save features that are new to Excel 97 and not supported by the earlier versions. ■

(See also "Opening: Files Saved in Other File Formats.")

Saving: Workspaces

You may have a group of workbooks that you use together, such as sales data from a number of different sales districts. Through the use of a *workspace* file, Excel enables you to save and then open multiple workbooks at a time when you start the program. When you save all open workbooks as a workspace file, Excel saves information such as the workbook names, screen locations, and window sizes. (See "Saving: Workbooks" before you complete this task.)

Steps

1. Open all the workbooks that you want to open together each time you start Excel.

2. Position the workbooks as you want them to appear in the workspace.

3. Choose File, Save Workspace. The Save Workspace dialog box appears.

4. In the Save In drop-down list, select the drive and folder

FILE MANAGEMENT

where you want to save the workspace.

5. In the File Name box, type a name for the workspace file; then click Save.

TIP To display the saved workspace each time you open Excel, save the workspace file in the Startup folder of the Excel (or Office) folder. If you prefer to open the workspace only when needed, save the file in a different folder. To open the workspace, choose File, Open; then select Workspaces in the Files of Type drop-down list, navigate to the workspace file location using the Look In list, select the file, and click Open.

NOTE When you open a workspace file, Excel opens each workbook you saved in the workspace. The workspace file doesn't contain the actual workbooks, however, so you must continue to save changes you make to the individual workbooks. ■

Shared Workbooks: Discontinuing Sharing

You can disable shared workbooks at any time. Before removing a workbook from shared use, you should ensure that you are the only user who has the workbook open. Otherwise, other users may lose their work. (See "Shared Workbooks: Setting Up" before you complete this task.)

CAUTION When you discontinue sharing a workbook, the change history is erased and cannot be viewed.

Steps

1. Open the workbook you want to discontinue sharing.

2. Choose Tools, Share Workbook; then click the Editing tab.

3. If other users are listed in the Who Has This Workbook Open Now list box, notify them to save and close the file.

4. Clear the Allow Changes by More Than One User at a

Time check box; then click OK.

5. In the message box that appears, click Yes to discontinue shared mode.

Shared Workbooks: Setting Up

If you are working on a network, Excel enables you to share your workbook with other users. When you enable the shared workbook capability, multiple users can view and modify a workbook simultaneously. Excel keeps track of who is currently accessing the workbook and what changes they make. The shared workbook feature is supported only by Excel 97. Users of previous versions of Excel cannot open shared workbooks.

Steps

1. With the workbook that you want to share active, choose Tools, Share Workbook; then click the Editing tab.

2. Select the Allow Changes by More Than One User at a Time check box; then click OK.

3. In the message box that appears, click OK to save the current workbook. The word (Shared) appears in the title bar.

4. Save the workbook in a location where others can access the file.

NOTE   When you save a shared workbook, you have two options for handling conflicting changes. You can have your changes replace the changes made by others, or you can review each change and decide to accept or reject the change. ■

(See also "Saving: Workbooks" and "Shared Workbooks: Discontinuing Sharing.")

Shared Workbooks: Viewing Changes

You can view a history of changes in a shared workbook in two different ways. The changes can appear highlighted on the

FILE MANAGEMENT

worksheet with details about the author, date, and time the changes were made displayed when you point to a revision. Or, the changes can be listed on a separate history worksheet. You can select both options, if you want. By default, Excel keeps a history of all the changes made in the past 30 days. This allows you to revert to a previous version of the shared workbook. (See "Shared Workbooks: Setting Up" and "Saving: Workbooks" before you complete this task.)

Steps

1. With the workbook that you want to share active, choose Tools, Track Changes, Highlight Changes.

2. Ensure that the Track Changes While Editing check box is selected. This enables workbook sharing as well as the change history.

3. In the Highlight Which Changes area, select the When check box, and then select All from the drop-down list.

4. Select the Highlight Changes on Screen check box if you want to see changes highlighted in the worksheet. Select the List Changes on a New Sheet check box if you want a list of changes to appear in a separate worksheet; this check box is available only after the workbook has been saved as a shared workbook.

5. Click OK; then save the workbook.

NOTE When you save a shared workbook, Excel removes the history information. To view the history information after you save the workbook, repeat the procedure in "Shared Workbooks: Viewing Changes" to display it again. ■

Workbooks: Adding Summary Information

You can enter summary information and other file properties for each workbook you create. In addition to documenting the workbook, the data you supply in the File Properties dialog box enables you to more easily locate a file at a later time (to do so, see "Files: Searching for Files").

Steps

1. With the workbook that you want to share active, choose File, Properties.

2. On the Summary tab, enter the summary information you want to save with the workbook. You can enter notes on a workbook in the Comments list box, for example.

3. Click the other tabs in the File Properties dialog box to add, edit, or view other information about the current workbook. Click OK when you have finished.

Workbooks: Closing a Workbook

When you have finished working with a workbook, you should close the workbook file to clear it from memory. You can close just the active workbook or all open workbooks at once.

Steps

1. If you want to close one workbook, display that workbook; then choose File, Close. If you want to close all open workbooks, hold down the Shift key, and then choose File, Close All. Holding down the Shift key toggles the File menu option between Close and Close All.

2. If you have made any changes to a workbook since it was opened or last saved, a dialog box prompts you to save the changed workbook. Click Yes to save changes and close the file; or click No to cancel changes and close the file; or click Cancel to return to the workbook.

Workbooks: Creating a New Workbook

When you start Excel, the program opens with a blank *workbook* on-screen, titled Book1. A workbook can contain one or more *sheets* of varying types. For example, a single workbook can include any of the following: worksheets, chart sheets, MS Excel 4.0 Macro sheets, and MS Excel 5.0 Dialog sheets. By default, a new workbook contains three worksheets.

When you use the File, New command to create a new workbook, you are prompted to select the template you want to use for the workbook. Most new workbooks that you create are based on the default Workbook template. You also can use any other available templates or create your own workbook template.

Steps

1. With Excel open, choose File, New.

2. Click the tab that contains the template you want, and then click the icon that represents the desired template. (The Workbook template on the General tab is the blank default template.) Click OK to create a new blank workbook.

TIP To quickly create a new workbook based on the default template, click the New button on the Standard toolbar.

TIP You can change the default number of worksheets that appears in a new workbook. Choose Tools, Options; then click the General tab. In the Sheets in New Workbook text box, type the number of worksheets you want new workbooks to contain; then click OK.

(See also "Customizing, Templates: Creating a Workbook Template" in this section and "Inserting Worksheets" in the "Editing Workbooks" section.)

Workbooks: Deleting a Workbook

If you no longer need a particular workbook, you can delete the entire workbook file. If you delete a workbook, you also delete all worksheets and other sheets (such as chart sheets) in that workbook. Excel prompts you for confirmation before deleting the workbook. You cannot delete a workbook currently open in Excel. (See also "Deleting: Worksheets" in the "Editing Workbooks" section.)

Steps

1. Make sure that the workbook you want to delete is closed; then choose File, Open to display the Open dialog box.

2. In the Look In drop-down list, select the drive and folder containing the workbook file you want to delete.

3. In the list box, right-click the file name of the workbook you want to delete.

4. Select Delete from the shortcut menu.

5. In the Confirm File Delete message box, click Yes to delete the file, or click No to return to the dialog box. Then click Cancel to close the dialog box.

Formatting

To enhance the appearance and improve readability of your worksheets, you can format the information in worksheet cells either before or after you enter the data. You can change the fonts or apply attributes such as boldface, italic, underline, borders, patterns, and colors. You also can apply numeric and date and time formats. Many of the formats you will use most often are accessible on the Formatting toolbar. Additional formatting options are available on the Format menu.

Alignment: Aligning Text Horizontally

Excel automatically aligns entries within a cell, according to the data you enter. When you enter text in a cell, Excel aligns the data to the left of the cell. When you enter numbers, Excel aligns them to the right. You can override this automatic alignment, however, and specify how you want data aligned: to the left, to the right, centered or justified within a cell, or centered across a range of cells.

In most cases, you will probably want to change the alignment of column headings so that the text is centered in each cell. If your worksheet data includes a title, you may also want to center the title over the worksheet data. (See also "Alignment: Centering Across Multiple Cells.")

Steps

1. Select the cell or range containing data you want to align. Choose Format, Cells; then click the Alignment tab.

2. Select one of the alignment options in the Horizontal drop-down list; then click OK.

You can quickly align data by selecting a cell or range, then clicking one of the following buttons on the Formatting toolbar: Align Left, Center, Align Right, or Merge and Center.

Alignment: Aligning Text Vertically

By default, Excel aligns text and numbers at the bottom edge of a cell. You can change the vertical alignment of cell data so that the data is displayed at the top edge or centered in a cell, or justified between the top and bottom edges. You may want to center text vertically in a cell, for example, if you want to place a border surrounding the cell.

Steps

1. Select the cell or range containing data you want to align. Choose Format, Cells; then click the Alignment tab.

2. Select one of the alignment options in the Vertical drop-down list; then click OK.

Alignment: Centering Across Multiple Cells

Excel enables you to center worksheet titles easily using two different methods. The Center Across Selection option in the Alignment tab of the Format Cells dialog box centers the title within a range of selected cells. You also can merge a range of selected cells into a single cell, and then center a title within the larger, merged cell. You can use the Merge and Center button on the Formatting toolbar to merge a selected range of cells and also center text within the new merged cell with a single mouse click.

When you merge a range of cells, the original cells become one large cell and you can no longer work in the individual cells. If your title is in cell A1, for example, you would select the range A1:A5 and click the Merge and Center button if you want the title to appear centered over the range A1:A5. After you merge the cells, the new merged cell is cell A1, and cells A2, A3, A4, and A5 no longer exist. An advantage to using the Merge Cells option is that you can align the contents in the merged cell any way you want. If you use the Center Across Selection option, however, you can only center text in the selected range. (See also "Alignment: Aligning Text Horizontally.")

Steps

1. Type and format the title in the left cell of the range in which you want the title centered. Select the cells across which you want the text centered.

2. Choose Format, Cells; then click the Alignment tab.

3. In the Horizontal drop-down list, select the Center Across Selection option; then click OK.

 To center a title using the Merge and Center button from the Formatting toolbar, type and format the title in the left cell of the range in which you want the title centered. Then, select the range and click the Merge and Center button.

If you later want to split a merged cell back into its individual cells, select the merged cell(s). Choose Format, Cells; then click the Alignment tab. Clear the Merge Cells check box; then click OK.

Alignment: Justifying Lines of Text

Excel's Justify option takes long strings of text, divides them into lengths that you specify, and reenters each length in its own cell (similar to full justification in a word processor). Lines are broken at spaces between words so that words stay together. The result appears as a paragraph with each new line starting in the next lower cell. You can use justification to join and wrap strings of text that are not in the same cell. (See also "Alignment: Aligning Text Horizontally.")

Steps

1. Select the range that contains the text you want to justify, and extend the range selection to the right and down to define how much space you want the text to occupy after justification.

2. Choose Format, Cells; then click the Alignment tab.

3. In the Horizontal drop-down list, select the Justify option; then click OK.

CAUTION   It is possible to overwrite existing text when you justify a range of data. If this happens, immediately choose Edit, Undo Justify. When you need more space to justify text, you can shorten the text, insert cells (or rows or columns) and select a larger area in which to justify the text, or move the obstructing information.

Alignment: Rotating Text

In Excel, the default orientation for text is horizontal, reading left to right. You can also align text so that the letters are stacked, reading top to bottom, or rotated anywhere from 90 degrees counterclockwise (reading sideways, bottom to top) to 90 degrees clockwise (reading sideways, top to bottom).

You can use rotated text effectively when you need vertical titles for reports or to label the sides of charts, tables, or drawings.

Steps

1. Select the cell or range containing data you want to rotate. Choose Format, Cells; then click the Alignment tab.

2. In the Orientation area, drag the pointer in the second box up or down to change the orientation of the text (as displayed in the Orientation preview box); or, specify a value in the Degrees box between 90 and –90 degrees. Then click OK.

TIP   To quickly select a stacked orientation, reading top to bottom, click the first box in the Orientation gauge; then click OK.

Alignment: Shrinking Text to Fit in a Cell

If you need to fit text in a cell without widening the column containing the text, you can shrink the size of the text by using the Shrink to Fit alignment option. If you apply the Shrink to Fit option to a cell and later add more text to the cell, Excel automatically shrinks the text more so that the text fits in the cell. If you delete some of the text from the cell, Excel increases the size of the text. (See also "Alignment: Wrapping Text in a Cell.")

Steps

1. Select the cell or range containing data you want to shrink. Choose Format, Cells; then click the Alignment tab.

2. Select the Shrink to Fit option; then click OK.

Alignment: Wrapping Text in a Cell

If you enter a long text entry in a cell, you can have Excel wrap the text so that it forms a paragraph that fits inside that cell. The cell's height increases to accommodate multiple lines of text. (See also "Alignment: Shrinking Text to Fit in a Cell.")

Steps

1. Select the cell or range containing data you want to wrap. Choose Format, Cells; then click the Alignment tab.

2. Select the Wrap Text option; then click OK.

TIP If you change the width of a column after you've wrapped text in that column, you may need to adjust the row height. Double-click the line just under the row number for the row containing the wrapped text to automatically adjust the row height.

Borders and Lines

You can place borders around cells, or use borders as lines and double lines under cells to add emphasis, to define data-entry areas, or to mark totals and subtotals. When combined with shading, borders make your worksheets easier to read and add interest. You can use the Borders button on the Formatting toolbar to quickly add borders to selected cells.

Steps

1. Select the cell or range to which you want to add a line or border.

2. Click the down arrow next to the Borders button on the Formatting toolbar. A palette of border selections appears. Click the desired border.

TIP You can access additional border options and line styles by using the Format Cells dialog box. First, select the cell or range where you want to add a border. Choose Format, Cells; then click the Border tab and select the options you want. If you want to add a color to your line or border, click the Color drop-down list and select a color from the palette.

Colors and Patterns

Just as fonts and attributes can enhance your worksheets, patterns and colors can help clarify meaning and make important data stand out by differentiating parts of the screen. If you have a color printer, you can print these colors.

Steps

1. Select the cell or range to which you want to add color or a pattern (or both). Choose Format, Cells.

2. Click the Patterns tab, and select the main color for your pattern from the Color grid. Select a pattern from the Pattern drop-down list.

3. If you want the pattern lines to appear in color (rather than black), select a color from the lower portion of the Pattern drop-down list. Check the Sample area at the

bottom-right corner of the dialog box to see the color and pattern; then click OK.

TIP Be careful not to use too many colors or patterns in a single worksheet, or you may distract the reader. Apply color or patterns sparingly, only to worksheet data you most want to emphasize.

You also can use buttons in the Formatting toolbar to change the color used for the cell background or the text in the cell. Select the cell or range you want to format. To change the background color, click the down arrow next to the Fill Color button; then click the color you want. To change the font color, click the down arrow next to the Font Color button; then click the color you want.

(See also "Formatting: Conditional Formats.")

Copying Formats with the Format Painter

You can use the Format Painter button in the Standard toolbar to copy formats such as font, style, alignment, borders, fills, and so on, from selected cells. This formatting can then be applied to any or all the other cells.

For example, if you normally use the same formats to indicate totals in your worksheets (such as boldface, underline, a larger font, and currency format), you can format just one total and then use the Format Painter to quickly copy all the formats from that cell to other cells within your worksheet.

Steps

1. Select the cell or range whose format(s) you want to copy.

2. Click the Format Painter button on the Standard toolbar. The pointer changes to a plus sign with a paintbrush attached.

3. Select the cell or range to which you want to copy the formats. The formatting is applied to the selected cell or range.

TIP If you want to "paint" the format to several cells or ranges, double-click the Format Painter button, and then select the cells or ranges. The Format Painter will remain active until you click the Format Painter button again or press Esc.

Fonts: Applying Boldface, Italic, and Underline

You can emphasize text in your worksheets by applying boldface, italic, or underline to cell data. For example, you can use boldface for titles and column headings, italic for key words or phrases, and underlines for totals. (See also "Borders and Lines.")

Steps

 1. Select the cell or range containing the text you want to format.

 2. Click the Bold, Italic, or Underline button in the Formatting toolbar. The new formatting appears in the cell.

 (See also "Formatting: Selected Characters in a Cell.")

Fonts: Changing Font Colors

With Excel, you can change the font colors that appear on-screen. If you have a color printer, you can print these colors.

Choose font colors carefully. From a readability standpoint, light font colors such as yellow are probably not a good choice—especially if you plan to present your worksheet data in an on-screen presentation. However, you may want to use lighter font colors if you also format the background of cells in a dark color (such as yellow text on a dark blue background). You should probably not use the color red to format numbers, unless you want to draw attention to negative numbers or perhaps sales figures that are below expectations. (See also "Colors and Patterns" and "Formatting: Conditional Formats.")

Steps

1. Select the cell or range containing the text you want to format.

2. Click the down arrow next to the Font Color button on the Formatting toolbar. A palette of colors appears.

3. Click the color you want to use. The selected text changes to the color you select.

TIP To see additional font colors, select the cell or range you want to format. Choose F<u>o</u>rmat, C<u>e</u>lls; then click the Font tab. Click the arrow beside the <u>C</u>olor drop-down list and choose the desired color; then click OK.

Fonts: Changing Fonts and Font Sizes

Fonts represent the various typefaces used in printed materials. These fonts may be changed to emphasize certain aspects of the data being presented. The height of fonts is measured in points; there are 72 points per inch. Therefore, an 18-point font will print 1/4 inch tall. You can also change the size of fonts. Some fonts are available in more sizes than other fonts. In general, it is probably best to avoid using more than three different fonts on a page of information, or the page may become too busy. (See also "Fonts: Applying Boldface, Italic, and Underline.")

Steps

1. Select the cell or range containing the text you want to format.

2. Click the down arrow next to the Font button on the Formatting toolbar. A list of available fonts appears. Click the font you want to use.

3. Click the down arrow next to the Font Size button on the Formatting toolbar. A list of available font sizes for the selected font appears. Click the font size you want to use.

TIP To apply other effects to fonts, such as strikethrough, superscript, or subscript formatting, choose F<u>o</u>rmat, C<u>e</u>lls; then click the Font tab. Select the desired options, and then click OK.

Formatting: Conditional Formats

A new feature in Excel 97 enables you to apply a specified format to cells, depending upon whether or not specific conditions in the cell are met. The value or contents in a cell is evaluated to determine whether the specified formatting should be applied. If the condition is met, you can specify that formatting such as font style, font color, cell color and pattern, and cell borders be applied to the cell.

Why Would I Use This?

Conditional formats are especially valuable when you need to check for data entry errors, evaluate analysis data, and verify data used in executive information systems.

In a sales worksheet, for example, you can format a cell so that data appears in red and boldface if the value in the cell falls below a specified amount, or blue if the cell's value exceeds a certain amount.

Steps

1. Select the cell to which you want to apply the conditional format; then, choose F<u>o</u>rmat, Con<u>d</u>itional Formatting.

2. Select Cell Value Is from the Condition drop-down list. Select one of the conditional operators, such as "greater than," from the next drop-down list.

3. Enter the values (or cell references) you want to compare in the two text boxes. Then, click the <u>F</u>ormat button and select the formatting you want to apply if the condition is met.

4. Click the <u>A</u>dd button if you want to add another condition, and then repeat steps 2 and 3. You can specify up to three conditions. Click OK.

To modify a conditional format, select the cells to which the conditional formatting has been applied, choose Format, Conditional Formatting, and modify the conditions and formatting as desired.

To delete a condition in a conditional format, click Delete in the Conditional Formatting dialog box to display the Delete Conditional Format dialog box. Select the conditions you want to delete and click OK.

NOTE If you want to format a cell based on a formula that you specify, select Formula Is in the Condition drop-down list. Then, enter a formula in the text box that appears. The formula must evaluate to TRUE or FALSE. If the formula evaluates to TRUE, the conditional format you specify is applied to the cell.

The formula can include references to cells in the worksheet to which you are applying the conditional formatting, but not references to other worksheets or workbooks. ■

TIP You can copy conditional formatting to other cells in the worksheet. Select the cell with the conditional format you want to copy, and then click the Format Painter button. Select the cells to which you want to copy the conditional formatting.

Formatting: Custom Numeric Formats

You can create your own custom numeric formats for financial or scientific tasks and create formats for catalog numbers, international currency, and so on. Any time you need to display a number in a special way, you should consider using a custom numeric format.

A custom format can have up to four parts, as shown in the following syntax line:

```
positive;negative;zero;text
```

You use a semicolon to separate the parts of a custom format.

The first position specifies the format for positive numbers in the cell, the second for negative numbers, and so on.

Steps

1. Select the cells for which you want to apply the custom format. Choose F̲ormat, C̲ells; then click the Number tab.

2. In the C̲ategory list, select Custom.

3. If an existing format closely resembles the custom format you want to create, select that format in the list.

4. In the T̲ype text box, edit the custom formats pattern. Click OK when you are done.

TIP   If you need help understanding the codes used in numeric formatting, press F1 while in the Format Cells dialog box; then choose the Help option related to custom format codes.

NOTE   Excel includes some Special formats for social security numbers, zip codes, and phone numbers. If this is the type of format you want to create, you may not need to create a custom format. Instead, select Special in the C̲ategory list, and then select the format you want. ■

To remove a custom format, choose F̲ormat, C̲ells; then click the Number tab. In the C̲ategory list, select Custom; then select the format you want to delete from the list and click D̲elete.

Formatting: Dates and Times

Regardless of how you enter or calculate the date and time, you can display the date and time using any of Excel's predefined formats. (See also "Entering: Dates and Times" in the section "Getting Started" and "Date and Time Functions" in the "Functions Mini-Reference" section.)

Excel supplies several predefined date and time formats for you. If you find that you want to use a format that isn't available, however, you can create a custom numeric format to display your date or time as you want it to appear. To do so, see "Formatting: Custom Numeric Formats" for more information.

Steps

1. Select the cell or range containing the date or time you want to format. Choose Format, Cells; then click the Number tab.

2. In the Category list, select either Date or Time.

3. Select the format you want from the Type list; then click OK.

Formatting: Multiple Worksheets

Excel enables you to perform operations to groups of worksheets at the same time. By grouping worksheets, you can save much formatting, data entry, and editing time by applying the same operations to the entire group at once. This is especially useful for applications such as consolidations, or worksheets that should contain common headings or formulas. If you name a range in the active sheet while sheets are grouped, the same name is applied to all the sheets in the group. You can only group worksheets that are contained in the same workbook. (See "Selecting: Worksheets" in the section "Getting Started" before you complete this task.)

Steps

1. Select the worksheets to which you want to apply identical formatting. Notice that the title bar now contains [Group].

2. Begin formatting one of the selected worksheets. All formatting you apply to the current worksheet also applies to other sheets in the group.

3. To separate the group into individual sheets, hold down the Shift key and click the sheet tab for the current worksheet.

Formatting: Numbers

By default, numbers are right-aligned and appear in the General number format. You can change the existing format to any Excel format you choose, however.(See also "Entering: Numbers" in the section "Getting Started.")

Excel supplies several predefined number formats for you. If you find that you want to use a format that isn't available, however, you can create a custom numeric format to display your number as you want it to appear in your worksheet. See "Formatting: Custom Numeric Formats" for more information.

Steps

1. Select the cell that contains the number. Choose Format, Cells; then click the Number tab.

2. Select the desired format from the Category list.

3. Choose from any additional options that appear (such as Decimal Places, if applicable); then click OK.

Formatting: Selected Characters in a Cell

You can apply one or more attributes, such as bold, italic, or underline, to individual characters within a cell rather than to the entire cell. If a cell entry contains two words, for example, you can apply formatting to only one of these words.

Steps

1. Select the cell containing the text you want to format. Select the text in the formula bar that you want to change by dragging across it with the mouse.

2. Choose Format, Cells. Select the options you want to change on the Font tab; then click OK.

Formatting: Tables with AutoFormats

Excel's *AutoFormat* feature lets you create professional-looking tables with the click of a few buttons. No matter what your level of expertise with Excel, you can use AutoFormat to apply a set of predefined formatting choices to reports, tables, and lists without resorting to complex formatting operations.

Steps

1. Select the range you want to format. Choose Format, AutoFormat.

2. In the Table Format list, select the desired format (a preview of your selection appears in the Sample box). Click OK. The range you selected now displays the AutoFormat you chose.

NOTE When you need to apply only parts of an AutoFormat, click the Options button in the AutoFormat dialog box. Clear formats in the Formats to Apply group that you do not want applied. For example, if you don't want AutoFormat to change your row heights or columns widths, clear the Width/Height check box. ■

TIP If the format does not appear as you expected, immediately choose Edit, Undo AutoFormat to restore the table to its previous format.

Hiding Zeros

Hiding zeros often makes detailed financial worksheets easier to read. You can choose to hide all zeros throughout the worksheet, or use a conditional format to specify a range of cells in which you want to hide zeros.

Steps

1. To hide zeros throughout the entire worksheet, choose Tools, Options; then click the View tab.

2. Clear the Zero Values check box; then click OK.

When you want to view the zeros again, select the Zero Values check box on the View tab.

TIP   You can use a conditional format to hide zeros by specifying white (or whatever the background color is, if it is not white) as the font color when the value of the cell equals zero. You can apply this format to the entire worksheet or to just a range of cells in which you want to hide zeros. (See "Formatting: Conditional Formats" for more information.)

Styles: Creating a Style

Styles are a set of predefined formats you can create and then apply to a cell or range. If you often format text as bold, italic, and right-aligned, for example, create a style that will assign each of these formats to a selected cell or range. The default (standard) format is stored in Excel's Normal style format. If you type data in an unformatted cell, Excel uses the Normal style for that cell.

Steps

1. Select a cell that contains the formatting to which you want to assign a style. Choose Format, Style. The Style dialog box appears.

2. In the Style Name list box, type a name for the new style. In the Style Includes area, select or clear the options, as desired.

3. Click the Modify button to display the Format Cells dialog box; select the desired formatting options, and then click OK to return to the Style dialog box.

4. Click the Add button to add the defined style to the list of styles; then click OK.

5. To use the style you created, select the cell or range you want to format. Choose Format, Style and select the style name from the Style Name list box; then click OK.

To delete a style you created, choose Format, Style. Then select the style name you want to delete in the Style Name list box and click the Delete button. Click OK. Any cells previously formatted with the style you deleted revert to the Normal style.

Styles: Merging Styles

If you've created styles in one workbook that you'd like to use in another workbook, you can copy the styles from one workbook to the other by merging the styles. All styles from the source workbook are merged into the target sheet–they will replace styles in the target sheet having the same name. (See "Styles: Creating a Style" before you complete this task.)

FORMATTING

Steps

1. Open the source and target workbooks and activate the workbook that will receive the copied styles.

2. Choose Format, Style; then click the Merge button.

3. In the Merge Styles From list, select the source workbook that contains the styles you want to copy; then click OK.

4. You may see an alert box if the source and target workbooks have styles with the same names. Select Yes if you want the source styles to replace styles with the same name in the target workbook; or select No if you want to merge all styles except those with the same name; or select Cancel if you don't want to merge any styles.

5. Excel returns you to the Style dialog box. Click the Close button.

Styles: Redefining Styles

Styles can save you time when you need to reformat a workbook. If your workbook uses styles, you need only to redefine the style. All cells in the workbook that use the style will immediately reformat to match the new style definition. Redefining the default Normal style affects all of the text in the current workbook that is not already formatted using other styles. (See "Styles: Creating a Style" before you complete this task.)

Steps

1. Open the workbook containing the style you want to redefine.

2. Choose Format, Style; then select the style you want to redefine in the Style Name list.

3. Click the Modify button; then select the tab for the type of formatting you want to redefine.

4. Change the formatting options for the style, as desired; then click OK.

5. Click OK to redefine the style and apply it to the current cell; or click Close to close the dialog box without applying the style to the selected cell.

Formula & Function Management

Formulas enable you to enter calculations in a worksheet. After you enter a formula, you can change the values in the referenced cells; Excel automatically recalculates values based on the cell changes.

Functions are predefined formulas that perform a specific operation, such as determining loan payments or calculating investment returns. Functions accept information, called *arguments*, and return a result. In most cases, the result is a calculation, but functions also return results that are text, references, logical values, arrays, or information about the worksheet.

For information on specific functions, refer to the "Functions Mini-Reference" located near the end of this book. This reference includes detailed information on many of the commonly used Excel functions from each of the function categories.

Auditing: Locating Errors in a Worksheet

Excel enables you to set up relationships among the various cells in the worksheet. However, if you run into an error in the worksheet, you may need to trace those various relationships to find the error. You can use the Auditing toolbar when you need to trace an error.

Examining the Error Values

Excel can display seven different types of error values. These error values are listed and described in the following table.

Excel Error Values

Error	Description
#DIV/0!	The formula is attempting to divide by zero. Check the cell references for blanks or zeros that may have resulted if you deleted a cell referenced by the formula.
#N/A	The formula refers to a cell with a #N/A entry or a cell that contains no value. This error value warns you that not all the data referenced by a formula is available.
#NAME?	Excel doesn't recognize a name you entered in a formula. Verify that all names used in the formula exist, and define any missing names. If applicable, verify that you used the correct function name.
#NULL!	The formula specifies two areas that don't intersect. Check to see if you entered the cell or range reference incorrectly. Remember to use commas (not spaces) between function arguments.
#NUM!	There is a problem with a number used in the formula. Check for the correct use of function arguments.
#REF!	A cell reference in the formula is incorrect. Check for changes to cell reference caused by deleting cells, rows, or columns referenced by the formula.
#VALUE!	The formula contains the wrong type of argument or operator. Check for the correct syntax of the formula.

Steps

1. To display the Auditing toolbar, choose Tools, Auditing, Show Auditing Toolbar.

2. Click the cell containing the error.

3. Click the Trace Error button on the Auditing toolbar. An arrow or arrows show the source of the error. Correct the error.

4. To remove the arrow(s), click the Remove All Arrows button on the Auditing toolbar.

Auditing: Tracing Formulas

You can display *tracer lines* to find *precedents* (cells that are referred to by a formula), *dependents* (cells that contain formulas that refer to other cells), and errors in any cell. Most of the time when you use the Auditing feature, you probably will want to trace the precedents to a formula to find out what other cells contribute to the formula in that cell. (See also "Auditing: Locating Errors in a Worksheet.")

Steps

1. To display the Auditing toolbar, choose Tools, Auditing, Show Auditing Toolbar.

2. Click the cell whose precedents you want to trace.

3. Click the Trace Precedents button on the Auditing toolbar. An arrow or arrows shows the precedents.

4. To remove the arrow(s), click the Remove Precedent Arrows button on the Auditing toolbar.

NOTE The *tracer lines* show the flow of data through the worksheet by connecting the active cell with related cells. The line ends with an arrow pointing to a formula. ■

TIP Double-click the arrow to go directly to the cell the arrow points to. Double-click the arrow a second time to highlight the formula precedents. This feature works as a toggle.

(See also "Formulas: Displaying Formulas.")

Formulas: Absolute, Relative, and Mixed Cell References

When a cell contains a formula with references to other cells, you can use several methods to handle those references. Each method causes a different result and may be utilized differently by Excel, so understanding the differences is important.

Understanding Cell Reference Types

Excel normally uses *relative references* for cell addresses in a formula, unless you specify otherwise. When you use relative references, the cell references in a formula automatically adjust after you copy the formula to another cell or range. If cell B10 contains the formula =SUM(B3:B9), for example, and you copy this formula from cell B10 to cell C10, the new formula in cell C10 automatically adjusts to read =SUM(C3:C9). In most cases, you want formulas to use relative cell references.

To prevent a cell reference in a formula from changing when you copy that formula to another cell or range, use an *absolute reference*. You indicate absolute references by typing a dollar sign ($) in front of the column letter and the row number. In a sales worksheet, for example, if you have a column of formulas that multiply a value by the commission percentage located in cell D7, you could use D7 to refer to that percentage in the first cell; then copy the formula down the column.

If you want only the row number or column letter (not both) to remain fixed when you copy a formula, use a *mixed reference* to refer to the cell address. The reference $C3 prevents the column from changing, for example, but the row changes relative to a new copied location. If you use C$3 as the reference, the column adjusts to a new location but the row remains fixed when you copy the formula.

(See "Formulas: Entering Formulas" before you complete this task.)

Steps

1. Place the cell pointer in the cell where you want to enter the formula.

2. To enter an absolute or mixed reference in a formula, type an equal sign (=) to start the formula (to enter a relative reference, just type the reference—no special treatment is needed). Then type or click the cell reference.

3. Press F4 until the desired combination of dollar signs appears, and then type the arithmetic operator, such as a plus sign (+).

4. Continue to type other values or cell references and operators as needed; then press Enter to complete the formula.

TIP You can use the F4 key to cycle between absolute, mixed, and relative references when editing an existing formula.

Formulas: Converting Formulas to Values

You can replace a formula in the worksheet with its calculated result if you no longer want or need to use the formula. When you convert the formula to a value, Excel permanently removes the formula (you can later reenter the formula if necessary).

For example, if you want to delete the cells or name to which a formula refers, first convert the formula to a value before deleting the cells or name. (See "Formulas: Entering Formulas" before you complete this task.)

Steps

1. Select the cell containing the formula you want to convert to a value.

2. Click the Copy button on the Standard toolbar.

3. Choose Edit, Paste Special, and then select the Values option. Click OK.

4. Press Enter to remove the marquee surrounding the cell.

Formulas: Creating a Text String

At times, you may need to create a formula that joins the contents of two cells. Excel refers to this action as *concatenation*.

How Concatenation Works

If a worksheet includes first names in one column and last names in another column, for example, you can enter a formula in a third column that joins the first name with the last name. Suppose that the first names are located in column B and the last names are located in column C; row 3 is the first row in the list. The following line shows an example of the formula for this situation:

=B3&" "&C3

The ampersand (&) in the preceding formula is the concatenation operator that joins text, numbers, and dates into one long text string. Note that if you used the formula =B3&C3 in this example, the first and last names would be joined together without a space. Therefore, you must use two quotation marks with a space between them (" ") to indicate that Excel should insert a space between the two text strings. (See "Formulas: Entering Formulas" before you complete this task.)

Steps

1. Select the cell where you want the formula to appear, and type an equal sign (=) to start the formula.

2. Type or click the first cell reference or name in the formula.

3. Type the concatenation operator (**&**), then type or click the next cell reference or name.

4. Repeat step 3 as necessary. Remember to type " " between the ampersands if you need to insert a space; press Enter to complete the formula.

(See also "Text Functions" in the "Functions Mini-Reference" section.)

Formulas: Displaying Formulas

You may at times prefer to see the formulas in your worksheets (such as =Jan+Feb) rather than the results of the formulas (such as 2,537). Perhaps you want to evaluate the structure of a worksheet to see that the formulas are correct, even if the worksheet contains no known errors. For example, you may notice incorrect cell references in displayed formulas that are causing inaccurate results (but not error values) in the worksheet.

Displaying all worksheet formulas also enables you to easily print all formulas used in the worksheet, for purposes of documentation. This step is a good safeguard in case you accidentally delete or lose the worksheet, or if the worksheet becomes damaged. (See "Formulas: Entering Formulas" before you complete this task.)

Steps

1. From anywhere in the worksheet, choose Tools, Options; then click the View tab.
2. Select the Formulas check box; then click OK.

To display the results again, choose Tools, Options; then clear the Formulas check box on the View tab.

TIP Press Ctrl+ ` (the grave accent, usually located on the same key as the tilde character) to toggle between viewing results and formulas.

Formulas: Entering Formulas

Formulas enable you to perform calculations by using values in the worksheet. When you use a formula to create a calculation, and you change any of the values referenced by the formula, Excel automatically recalculates the result. You can enter formulas in two ways: type the formula directly in the cell, or point to the cells that you want the formula to compute. Arithmetic operators that you can use in formulas are listed in the following table. (See also "Functions: Entering Functions.")

FORMULA/FUNCTION MANAGEMENT

Arithmetic Operators

Operator	Description
+ (plus sign)	Addition
– (minus sign)	Subtraction
* (asterisk)	Multiplication
/ (slash)	Division
% (percent symbol)	Percentage
^ (caret)	Exponentiation

Steps

1. Select the cell where you want the formula to appear, and type an equal sign (=) to start the formula.
2. Type or click the first cell reference in the formula. (You also can type a value or name.)
3. Type the arithmetic operator, such as a plus sign (+). Refer to the preceding table for a list of other arithmetic operators.
4. Type or click the next cell reference.
5. Repeat steps 3 and 4 as necessary; then press Enter to complete the formula.

The cell displays the formula result. When you select the cell containing the formula, you see the formula in the formula bar.

TIP Instead of typing an equal sign in step 1 of the preceding steps, you can click the Edit Formula button (the **=** in the formula bar). If you click the Edit Formula button, Excel automatically inserts an equal sign and displays the results of the formula as you enter it. When you are done, click OK or press Enter to complete the formula.

NOTE Many formula errors occur when the arithmetic operators are not entered in the proper order in which Excel performs the operations. Exponentiation occurs before multiplication and division, and multiplication and division occur before addition and subtraction. This is sometimes called the order of precedence. You can alter this order by enclosing segments of a formula in parentheses. For example, in the formula =3*(7+5), you force Excel to add 7 and 5, and then multiply that result by 3. ■

(See also "Naming Cells and Ranges" in the "Getting Started" section.)

Formulas: Filling Cells by Using Ctrl+Enter

You can use Ctrl+Enter to quickly fill cells as you enter data or formulas. When you press Ctrl+Enter, formulas and values fill into all selected cells just as though you used a Fill or Copy and Paste command. This method also works with nonadjacent multiple selections. (See "Formulas: Entering Formulas" before you complete this task.)

Steps

1. Select the adjacent cells or ranges you want to fill.

2. With the range(s) still selected, type the formula or value in the active cell.

3. Press Ctrl+Enter (rather than just Enter) to enter the formula or value.

Formulas: Referencing Cells in Other Worksheets

You can refer to other sheets in a workbook by including a sheet reference as well as a cell reference in a formula. To refer to cell C7 on Sheet3, for example, type **Sheet3!C7** in the formula. Use an exclamation mark (!) to separate the sheet reference from the cell reference. If you have named the sheet, simply use the sheet name and then the cell reference, such as Details!C7. If the sheet name includes spaces, you must surround the sheet reference with single quotation marks, such as 'Sales Details'!C7. (See "Formulas: Entering Formulas" before you complete this task.)

FORMULA/FUNCTION MANAGEMENT

Steps

1. Select the cell where you want the formula to appear, and type an equal sign (=) to start the formula.

2. Click the sheet tab containing the cell you want to reference in the formula.

3. Select the cell or range you want to refer to. The complete reference appears in the formula bar.

4. Finish the rest of the formula; then press Enter to complete the formula.

(See also "Linking: Cells by Pointing" in the section "Linking and Embedding.")

Formulas: Unprotecting and Hiding

Cell protection prevents someone from accidentally entering data on top of a formula and prevents unauthorized users from changing your formulas. You also can specify whether a cell's contents are visible in the formula bar. Even when the cell contents are hidden from the formula bar, however, the cell's value or formula results still appear in the worksheet. (See "Formulas: Entering Formulas" in this section and "Protecting: Cell Data" in the section "Editing Workbooks" before you complete this task.)

Steps

1. To unprotect a cell so that it can be changed or to hide a cell's contents from the formula bar, select the cell or range that you want to unprotect or whose contents you want to hide from the formula bar.

2. Choose Format, Cells; then click the Protection tab.

3. Clear the Locked check box to mark the cell or range as one that can be changed, or select the Hidden check box to mark the cell or range as one whose contents do not show in the formula bar; then click OK.

4. You can continue to change all cells in the worksheet and see any cell contents until you turn on protection for the worksheet. Protection and hiding do not take effect until you use the Tools, Protection command.

Functions: Entering Functions

You can enter functions manually if you know the function name and what data to supply for the arguments in a function. In most cases, you will probably type only simple functions that require one argument, such as a range of data. For more complex functions that require multiple arguments, you can use the Paste Function. (See "Functions: Inserting with the Paste Function.")

Steps

1. Select the cell where you want the function to appear, and type an equal sign (=) to start the function.

2. Type the function name (such as **AVERAGE**) and a left parenthesis.

3. Select the range of cells for the argument and press Enter. Excel automatically adds the closing parenthesis and enters the function.

Functions: Inserting with the Paste Function

The *Paste Function* displays a list of functions from which you can choose the function you want, based on a description that appears when you select a function. The Paste Function also assists you in building the function and explains the purpose of each argument in a function.

Use the Paste Function if you want to enter a complex function that requires multiple arguments or if you are unsure of the syntax required for a specific function. (See also "Functions: Entering Functions.")

Steps

1. Select the cell where you want to enter the function, then click the Paste Function button on the Standard toolbar.

2. Select the type of function you want from the Function Category list. If you are unsure of the category, select Most Recently Used or All.

3. Choose the specific function that you want from the Function Name list box. Read the description in the lower part of the dialog box to verify that this is the function you want; then click OK.

4. A pop-up window, called the *Formula Palette*, appears under the formula bar. Enter the arguments in each argument text box. You can type the cell references or numbers, click the cell to enter, or drag across multiple cells to enter.

5. Click OK to complete the function and insert it in the cell.

Totals: AutoCalculate

If you need to find a quick total in a worksheet, but you don't want or need to include that total in the worksheet, you can use the *AutoCalculate* feature. For example, you may want to sum a list and then use that sum in a formula. You could grab a calculator and add up the figures using the calculator. Or you can use Excel's AutoCalculate feature.

Steps

1. Select the range you want to sum. The AutoCalculate button in the status bar automatically displays the sum of the selected range.

2. Right-click the AutoCalculate button in the status bar.

3. From the pop-up menu that appears, select the function you want to use, such as Average or Count. The result of the function you selected appears in the status bar.

If you select additional ranges, Excel uses the most recent function you selected on the AutoCalculate button.

Totals: AutoSum

The SUM function totals the numeric value of all cells in the range(s) it references. An *AutoSum* button, which you can use to sum adjacent columns or rows automatically, appears on the

Standard toolbar. In addition to entering the SUM function automatically, the AutoSum button selects the cells in the column above or in the row to the left of the current cell.

Steps

1. Select a cell below or to the right of the values you want to sum.

2. Click the AutoSum button on the Standard toolbar.

3. To accept the formula that AutoSum supplies, press Enter. Or, if the formula is incorrect, select a different range to sum and then press Enter.

NOTE   If you select a range of cells and then click the AutoSum button, Excel automatically enters the formula results for the entire range. ■

Totals: Creating and Removing

Subtotals are a quick and easy way to summarize data in an Excel list. Suppose you have a list of sales information that includes the date, account, product, unit, price, and revenue. You can specify that you want to see subtotals by account, or subtotals by product, and so on.

With Excel's Subtotals command, you don't need to create the formulas. Excel creates the formula, inserts the subtotal row(s), and outlines the data automatically. The resulting data is easy to format, chart, and print.

Steps

1. Sort the list as you want and click a cell in the column that you want to subtotal; then choose Data, Subtotals.

2. In the Subtotal dialog box, make any changes you want. To create subtotals for more than one column, for example, select additional columns in the Add Subtotal To list.

3. Click OK. Excel creates the subtotals; a grand total appears at the bottom of the list.

FORMULA/FUNCTION MANAGEMENT

TIP To quickly remove the subtotals from your list, select a cell in the list. Then choose Data, Subtotals, and click Remove All.

CAUTION Excel lists work best when it can readily distinguish the column labels and data entries in the list. Include a row of column labels across the top and, with no blank rows, place your data in the appropriate columns just below the labels.

Totals: Creating Nested Subtotals

If you want additional subtotals within each group (nested subtotals), you can create two sets of subtotals. For instance, you might want to total all accounts and also include subtotals for each product within an account.

Steps

1. Sort the list by the two or more columns that you want to contain subtotals. Click a cell in the first column you want to subtotal.

2. Choose Data, Subtotals; then click OK to insert subtotals for your first sorted column.

3. Click a cell in the second column you want to subtotal.

4. Choose Data, Subtotals; then choose the options for the second group.

5. In the At Each Change In drop-down list, select the column for the second set of subtotals. Then clear the Replace Current Subtotals check box and click OK.

Totals: Multiple Summary Functions

In addition to the SUM function (used for creating subtotals in Excel lists), a number of other Excel functions are useful in lists. For instance, you may want to use COUNT to summarize the number of items in the list, AVERAGE to give the average values in the list, and MAX to give the largest value in a list.

Steps

1. To display two or more summary functions for the same set of data, first choose Data, Subtotals.

2. Select the first function in the Use Function drop-down list; then click OK. Excel inserts the subtotal rows.

3. Choose Data, Subtotals (again) and then select another function from the Use Function drop-down list.

4. Clear the Replace Current Subtotals check box; then click OK. Excel inserts an additional subtotal row with the new calculation.

FORMULA/FUNCTION MANAGEMENT

Linking and Embedding

Object Linking and Embedding (OLE) enables you to create work in one application and share that work with another application. You can use the numbers in a worksheet to create a table in a printed report; import a database table for use in Excel; or even combine the contents of many kinds of documents, in many different applications, to create an annual report. Object linking and object embedding are two related techniques that seem to accomplish similar goals. The main difference between linking and embedding is where the data is stored.

Linked data is stored in a source file. When you link an object, a copy of the original data appears in the second (destination) application; the original data remains intact in the first (source) application. If you use object linking to copy a table of numbers from Excel to Word, for example, the data remains in Excel, but a copy of the table also appears in Word. To change the table in Word, you return to Excel and change the original numbers. Because a link has been set up between the two applications, any changes to the data in Excel change the table in Word.

Embedded objects become part of the destination document. When you embed an object, you create the object in the source application as you do when linking; however, there is only one copy of the object and that resides within the destination document. You can embed an Excel chart in a Word document. In Word, you create the object using Excel menus and tools. You then update the object and exit Excel. When you want to edit the embedded object, you double-click the chart in Word to open the Excel window in which the object resides.

In OLE 2, which is a more recent version of OLE, you also can drag and drop shared data between open applications. OLE 2 makes it easier to edit the objects you link and embed. Suppose you create a worksheet in Excel that you embed into a Word report. When you edit the worksheet from Word, OLE 2 provides appropriate Excel menus that enable you to edit the worksheet more quickly and easily than if you switch to the actual source program. Many of the applications you use in Windows 95, such as Excel 97 and Word 97, use OLE 2.

NOTE   The general techniques you learn in this section apply to other Microsoft Office applications (such as Word, PowerPoint, and Access) as well as Windows applications from other software developers (such as Excel, WordPerfect, and Approach) that support OLE. Consult the user manual for the application to see whether it is OLE-compatible. ■

Cell Pictures: Capturing a Picture of Cells

If you want to create a worksheet displaying ranges of data from multiple worksheets, you can capture a picture of the ranges from each worksheet and combine them onto one worksheet as linked objects. You also can use these captured cell pictures in other Office applications, such as Microsoft Word.

Capturing cell pictures provides several advantages over creating formula links to cells in other worksheets. The linked cell pictures can be opened and updated quickly—you can double-click the cell picture to access and modify the source information. Linked cell pictures are actually objects that can easily be moved or resized, which facilitates layout. In addition, you can format linked cell pictures by using many of the same features as text boxes.

The cell picture includes only the visible information in the captured cells, including cell gridlines. You may want to omit the gridlines before you capture the picture (see "Hiding: Gridlines" in the "Customizing" section). You also may want to resize columns or rows before capturing the cell picture in order to improve the appearance of the linked picture (see "Adjusting: Column Widths" and "Adjusting: Row Heights" in the "Editing Workbooks" section).

Steps

1. In the source worksheet, select the range of cells you want to create a picture from, and click the Copy button on the Standard toolbar.

2. Select the destination worksheet (or other document) where you want to paste the picture.

3. Hold down the Shift button, then choose Edit, Paste Picture Link. The pasted cells now appear as an object in the destination worksheet.

4. Move or size the object, as desired.

TIP If you want to copy the picture to a document in another Office application, copy the Excel range to the Clipboard; then choose Edit, Paste Special in the other application. Click Paste Link; then in the As list box, select Picture. Click OK.

Cell Pictures: Updating Linked Cell Pictures

You can update information in the source worksheet that contains the data linked to a cell picture, and have those changes reflected immediately in the cell picture. You don't need to remember where the source data is located, because you can activate the source worksheet directly from the cell picture. This feature is especially convenient if you need to update several cell pictures contained in the same worksheet. (See "Cell Pictures: Capturing a Picture of Cells" before you complete this task.)

Steps

1. Open the worksheet (or other Office document) containing the cell picture; then double-click the picture. Excel opens the source worksheet and selects the range that is linked to the picture.

2. Make any desired changes to the source worksheet, and then save the source worksheet. The changes are reflected in the linked cell picture.

Dragging Data between Programs

You can use the mouse to move or copy information from one application to another using a simple drag-and-drop operation, as long as both applications support OLE.

Steps

1. Open both the source and destination applications; position the applications so that you can see the area you want to copy from and the area you want to paste to.

2. Select the data in the source application that you want to move or copy to the destination application.

3. To move the selection, drag it to the destination application and drop it where you want the data to appear. To copy the selection, hold down the Ctrl key while you drag and drop.

 TIP To more easily arrange the two applications on-screen, minimize all applications except the two you are working with. Right-click in the Windows taskbar and choose either Tile Horizontally or Tile Vertically.

Embedding: Editing Linked and Embedded Objects

When you link or embed an object in an Excel worksheet, you can edit the object or the linked data using the data's original application. This enables you to use features designed for this specific type of data. You can edit a linked object by changing and then updating the original object or by editing the link itself.

Objects linked into Excel update automatically, by default. When you change the source document and save the file, the object embedded in Excel updates to reflect the change.

Steps

1. To edit the object, double-click it. The source application reopens, with the object on-screen.

2. Edit the object, as desired.

3. Click outside the source application when you are done, to return to the worksheet and restore the Excel menus and toolbars.

 TIP To quickly access all the commands that apply to an embedded object, right-click the object to display the object's shortcut menu.

Embedding: Including Data from Other Applications

After you embed data from another application into Excel, the data is part of the Excel worksheet. You can edit the embedded data by starting the other application from within Excel. You can embed an object into an Excel document in two ways: by using the Insert command and creating the embedded object from within Excel; or by opening an application that contains an existing object, and then copying and pasting the object into Excel. Objects you embed in Excel appear as pictures that you can resize and move.

Steps

1. To insert a new embedded object into Excel, open the worksheet where you want the object to appear and choose Insert, Object; then click the Create New tab.

2. In the Object Type list, select the source application you want to use; then click OK. The source application opens.

3. Create the object, using the source application; then, click outside of the source application area.

4. If a confirmation dialog box appears, click Yes.

LINKING AND EMBEDDING

Linking: Cells by Pointing

If you need to create links to individual cells or links within formulas, you can use the pointing method to create the links. You can point to cells in other workbooks and create the links, just as you can point to any cell in the current workbook. To point to a cell so that it is included in a formula, click it as you build the formula.

Steps

1. Open the destination and source workbooks; then activate the destination workbook.

2. Select the cell that you want to contain the link and start the formula. The formula can include several terms or can just use an equal sign (=) and the single linked cell.

3. Activate the source workbook; then select the source cell or range that supplies data to the link.

4. Continue building the formula. After you complete the formula, press Enter.

(See also "Formulas: Entering Formulas" in the "Formula & Function Management" section.)

Linking: Cells with Copy and Paste Link

You can link an Excel cell or range in a source workbook to a cell or range in a destination workbook by using the Copy and Paste Link commands. The Paste Special dialog box used in this procedure enables you to choose which components of a cell or range you want to paste link, such as all, formulas, values, or formats. You also can specify a mathematical operation to perform on the link, if desired.

Steps

1. Open the destination and source workbooks; then activate the source workbook.

 2. Select the range of cells that provide the data you want linked; then choose <u>E</u>dit, <u>C</u>opy.

3. Activate the destination workbook; then click the top-left cell of the range where you want the link to appear.

4. Choose Edit, Paste Special. The Paste Special dialog box appears.

5. In the Paste area, select All; in the Operation area, select None. Then click the Paste Link button.

Linking: Excel Data with Other Windows Applications

Through object linking, a Windows application can send data to or receive data from another Windows application that is capable of OLE. Excel can create links by using its Edit, Copy and Paste Special commands as long as the other Windows application also has OLE commands available. In this case, creating object links between two Windows applications is as easy as linking two worksheets.

Steps

1. Open Excel and the other Windows application; then display the source application.

2. Select the text, cell, range, value, graphic object, or data that you want to link.

3. Choose Edit, Copy.

4. Switch to the destination application and select where you want the linked data to appear.

5. Choose Edit, Paste Special; then select Paste Link. Click OK.

NOTE If the Paste Link option is not available in the Edit menu after you copy data from another Windows application to Excel, the source application doesn't support OLE through menus; you cannot paste the link into Excel. ▨

Linking: Opening Linked Workbooks

When you open a workbook containing linked data, you update the linked data in different ways. If the source workbook is already open, the destination workbook automatically updates when you open it. If the source workbook is not open when you open the destination workbook, you can choose to keep the old values or update links to files on disk.

Steps

1. Open the destination workbook that contains the links, and choose Edit, Links.

2. In the Source File list, select the files you want to open. To select multiple files, hold down the Ctrl key and click each file. Unopened files appear with their path name.

3. To complete the update process, click the Open Source button.

NOTE   Be sure that the destination workbook is the active workbook. If a workbook without links is active, the Edit, Links command is unavailable. ■

Linking: Updating and Changing Linked Workbooks

To maintain linked workbooks, you need to know how to re-establish lost links and how to update links. If you rename or move source workbooks to different folders, destination workbooks cannot automatically find the new location of the source data. These links must be reestablished.

Steps

1. Open the destination workbook that contains the links; then choose Edit, Links.

2. In the Source File list, select the files you want to update or change. Unopened files appear with their path name. Click the Change Source button; the current link is displayed at the top of the Change Links dialog box.

3. Select a folder and file name for the new supporting workbook, or type the folder and file name of the file you want to establish as the source.

4. Click OK to link to the file name you selected, or click Cancel to ignore the change.

5. If you selected multiple source files in step 2 above, repeat steps 3 and 4 for each workbook.

 TIP   To update an active destination workbook if the source workbook is unopened, choose Edit, Links. Then, select the source workbook and click the Update Now button.

Producing Output

Excel provides several methods of producing output for your data. After you preview your data and adjust the page setup options as necessary, you can send the data directly to a printer. You can print a selected range, a selected chart, or an entire worksheet. If you print the same area of a worksheet on a regular basis, you can define that range as a print area, and print the range without having to respecify the print area each time.

In addition, you can fax or e-mail your data from Excel, or publish your Excel worksheets on the Web.

Page Setup: Creating Headers and Footers

You can add information to the top and bottom margins of the printed page to help document your printed worksheets. You can include such information as the current date and time, the file name, and the current page number. Excel provides pre-defined headers and footers, and also enables you to create custom headers and footers.

Steps

1. With the worksheet open, choose File, Page Setup; then click the Header/Footer tab.

2. Click the arrow beside the Header drop-down list to see the predefined header options; choose the desired header, or choose (none) if you do not want to display a header. Or if you want to create a custom header, click the Custom Header button and enter the desired header or footer information in the Left Section, Center Section, and Right Section text boxes; then click OK.

3. Click the arrow beside the Footer drop-down list to see the predefined footer options and choose the desired footer, or choose (none) if you do not want to display a footer. Or if you want to create a custom footer, click the Custom Footer button and enter the desired header or footer information in the Left Section, Center Section, and Right Section text boxes; then click OK.

5. Click Print Preview to preview the current print settings; then click Print if you want to print the worksheet now, or click Close to return to the worksheet.

TIP   Headers and footers automatically print one-half inch from the top or bottom of the paper, unless you change the header or footer distance from the edge of the page. Use the Header and Footer options on the Margins tab of the Page Setup dialog box to change these settings.

Page Setup: Fitting a Document to a Page

You can use Excel settings to proportionally reduce or enlarge the printed worksheet. Use the Fit To option if you want to scale the printed worksheet to a specified number of pages.

The Fit To option is frequently used when a portion of a worksheet prints on a second page and you prefer the entire worksheet to print on a single page. (See also "Page Setup: Reducing and Enlarging Printouts.")

Steps

1. With the worksheet open, choose File, Page Setup; then click the Page tab.

2. In the Scaling area, select the Fit To option.

3. If you want the worksheet to print on more than one page wide or one page tall (the defaults), change these options in the text boxes beside the Fit To option.

4. Click Print Preview to preview the current print settings; then click Print if you want to print the worksheet now, or click Close to return to the worksheet.

Page Setup: Reducing and Enlarging Printouts

You can use the Adjust To option if you want to print the worksheet full size or scale the worksheet to a specified percentage of full size.

By default, a worksheet prints at 100% (normal size). If your printer is not capable of scaling the print job to fit the page, the Adjust To and Fit To boxes are unavailable. (See also "Page Setup: Fitting a Document to a Page.")

Steps

1. With the worksheet open, choose File, Page Setup; then click the Header/Footer tab.

2. Enter the desired size in the Adjust To text box. If you enter a number smaller than 100, the page is reduced to that percentage of the original. If you enter a number larger than 100, the page is enlarged.

3. Click Print Preview to preview the current print settings; then click Print if you want to print the worksheet now, or click Close to return to the worksheet.

Page Setup: Setting a Print Area

If you want to print a portion of an Excel worksheet rather than the entire worksheet, you first should define the area you want to print.

Steps

1. Select the range of data in the worksheet that you want to print.

2. Choose File, Print Area, Set Print Area. A dotted line indicates the selected print area in the worksheet.

3. If you later want to clear the predefined print area, choose File, Print Area, Clear Print Area.

 TIP After you define a print area, you can click the Print button on the Standard toolbar to print that worksheet area.

(See also "Printing: Worksheet Data.")

Page Setup: Setting Manual Page Breaks

When you preview and print worksheet data, Excel automatically inserts page breaks for you. You can, however, insert and remove manual page breaks wherever you want.

Steps

1. To insert a vertical page break, click the column heading just to the right of where the page break should appear. To insert a horizontal page break, click the row heading just below where the page break should appear.

   To insert both vertical and horizontal page breaks simultaneously, select the cell just to the right and just below where you want the page breaks to appear.

2. Choose Insert, Page Break. A dashed line in the worksheet indicates the position of the page break.

To remove a manual page break, select a cell adjacent to the page break. Then choose Insert, Remove Page Break.

Page Setup: Setting Margins

By default, Excel prints a worksheet with 1-inch margins at the top and bottom, and 3/4-inch margins on the left and right sides of the worksheet. You can use the Page Setup dialog box to change these margins, if necessary. If your worksheet is small, for example, you may want to increase the margins or specify that you want the worksheet data centered on the page. In most cases, this will improve the appearance of the printed data.

Steps

1. With the worksheet open, choose File, Page Setup; then click the Margins tab.

2. In the Top, Left, Bottom, and Right text boxes, specify the margins you want, in inches.

3. If you want to center the worksheet on the printed page, select Horizontally and/or Vertically.

4. Click Print Previe̲w to preview the current print settings; then click P̲rint if you want to print the worksheet now, or click C̲lose to return to the worksheet.

Page Setup: Setting Multiple Print Areas

You can specify multiple print ranges in the worksheet, which Excel can then print by using a single print command. Use this technique if you need to create a single printed report from different areas of a worksheet. Each print area you select prints on a separate page.

Steps

1. With the worksheet open, choose F̲ile, Page Setu̲p; then click the Sheet tab.

2. Select the Print A̲rea text box, then select the first range in the worksheet that you want to print. (If necessary, drag the Page Setup dialog box out of the way.)

3. Type a comma (,) in the Print A̲rea text box, and then select the next range you want to print. Select the ranges in the order that you want them to print.

4. Repeat Step 3 until you have selected all the areas you want to print.

5. Click Print Previe̲w to preview the current print settings; then click P̲rint if you want to print the worksheet now, or click C̲lose to return to the worksheet.

TROUBLESHOOTING   **When I select multiple print ranges, each range prints on a separate page. How can I print multiple print ranges on a single page?** You can temporarily hide the rows and columns that separate the ranges and then print them as one print range (see "Hiding: Columns and Rows" in the section "Editing Workbooks"). Or, you can copy the ranges you want to print to another worksheet, and then print the copied data as a single print range (see "Copying: Cell Data" in the section "Editing Workbooks").

Page Setup: Setting the Orientation

If the worksheet you want to print is wider than it is tall, you may want to switch to a landscape orientation when you print. Choose Landscape orientation to print the worksheet across the long edge of the page. Use Portrait orientation (the default) to print across the short edge of the page.

Steps

1. With the worksheet open, choose File, Page Setup; then click the Page tab.

2. In the Orientation area, select Portrait or Landscape.

3. Click Print Preview to preview the current print settings; then click Print if you want to print the worksheet now, or click Close to return to the worksheet.

 TIP If your printer can print using different paper sizes, you may want to print some worksheets on legal-sized paper (or another size paper, such as envelopes) rather than the standard letter-sized worksheets. Select the Paper Size option on the Page tab to access the available paper sizes for the selected printer.

Previewing a Workbook

Before you print a worksheet, you should preview it to see how the worksheet will look when printed. (See "Page Setup: Setting a Print Area" before you complete this task.)

Steps

1. With the worksheet you want to preview active, click the Print Preview button on the Standard toolbar. The Preview window appears.

2. Choose from the available buttons at the top of the Preview window. For example, click Setup to change page setup options, or click Zoom to zoom in on the worksheet.

3. Click Close to return to the normal worksheet view.

NOTE You also can access the Preview window by clicking the Print Preview button in the Page Setup dialog box or the Preview button in the Print dialog box. ■

Printing: Multiple Copies

Before you begin printing your worksheet, you can specify how many copies of the worksheet you want to print. If you want to print multiple copies of a multi-page worksheet, be sure to preview the worksheet before you print it.

You also can choose whether or not to collate the numbered pages in a worksheet when you print multiple copies of a worksheet. Normally, you will want to choose the Collate option, which prints all pages of a worksheet before it prints the worksheet again. If this option is not selected, the first page prints for all copies, then the second page prints for all copies, and so on. (See "Page Setup: Setting a Print Area" and "Previewing a Workbook" before you complete this task.)

Steps

1. With the worksheet open, choose File, Print and then type the number of copies you want to print in the Number of Copies text box.

3. Be sure that the Collate check box is selected; or, if you don't want your printouts to collate, deselect the Collate check box; then click OK to begin printing.

Printing: Repeating Titles

In a multiple-page printout, you may want to repeat row or column titles on each page to make the printout easier to read. If a worksheet is wider than one page, for example, you can repeat row titles along the left margin of each page. You also can repeat column titles at the top of each page of a multiple-page worksheet. (See "Page Setup: Setting a Print Area" before you complete this task.)

Steps

1. With the worksheet open, choose File, Page Setup; then click the Sheet tab.

2. In the Print Titles area, select either the Rows to Repeat at Top check box or the Columns to Repeat at Left check box.

3. In the worksheet, select the row(s) or column(s) of titles you want to appear on each printed page. The rows or columns you select must be adjacent.

4. Click Print Preview to preview the current print settings; then click Print if you want to print the worksheet now, or click Close to return to the worksheet.

NOTE If the rows or columns you specify as print titles also appear in the range you've selected as the print area, you may see two sets of the rows or columns when you print the worksheet. To avoid this problem, respecify the print area so that it doesn't include addresses for the row or column print titles. ■

To delete the repeating titles if you no longer want to use them, choose File, Page Setup, click the Sheet tab, and then clear the Rows to Repeat at Top and Columns to Repeat at Left text boxes.

Printing: Row and Column Headings

For most worksheets you print in Excel, you don't need to print the row and column headings (the row numbers and column letters) with the worksheet data. However, you may want to use this option to help document a worksheet you created. You can, for example, display the formulas in a worksheet, and then print the data with the row and column headings so that you can immediately see where each of the formulas is located. This can prove to be a valuable tool for auditing worksheet formulas as well as documenting the worksheet. (See "Formulas: Displaying Formulas" in the section "Formula & Function Management" and "Page Setup:

Setting a Print Area" in this section before you complete this task.)

Steps

1. With the worksheet open, choose File, Page Setup; then click the Sheet tab.

2. In the Print area, select the Row and Column Headings check box.

3. Click Print Preview to preview the current print settings; then click Print if you want to print the worksheet now, or click Close to return to the worksheet.

Printing: Worksheet Data

After you've created a worksheet and have entered and formatted your data, you usually want to print the data and distribute the printouts to others. As described throughout this part of the book, Excel provides many printing features that enable you to enhance the appearance of your printouts. You should preview the worksheet data and adjust the page setup options as necessary before you actually print the worksheet. (See also "Previewing a Workbook.")

Steps

1. Select the range of data in the worksheet that you want to print, and choose File, Print.

2. In the Print Range and Print What areas, select the area you want to print. If you already selected a print range in Step 1 above, be sure to choose Selection in the Print What area, if necessary.

3. Click Preview to preview the current print settings; then click Print if you want to print the worksheet now, or click Close to return to the worksheet.

 TIP   To begin printing the worksheet data immediately using the default print settings, select the range you want to print and then click the Print button in the Standard toolbar.

Printing: Worksheet Gridlines

You can choose to print both vertical and horizontal gridlines with your worksheet data when you print the data. Gridlines will print around each cell in the worksheet range, regardless of whether or not the cell contains data. This feature is useful when printing large worksheets with multiple columns and rows of numeric data, so you can more easily see which column and row headings apply to each number. (See "Page Setup: Setting a Print Area" before you complete this task.)

Steps

1. With the worksheet open, choose File, Page Setup; then click the Sheet tab.

2. In the Print area, select the Gridlines check box.

3. Click Print Preview to preview the current print settings; then click Print if you want to print the worksheet now, or click Close to return to the worksheet.

NOTE   Do not confuse the on-screen display of gridlines in the worksheet with printed gridlines. Even if you see gridlines displayed in the worksheet, you still must select the Gridlines check box in the Page Setup dialog box in order to print gridlines.

TIP   If you only want to print vertical *or* horizontal lines (not both), or if you want to choose exactly where you want lines to appear in a printed worksheet, you should add borders or lines to the worksheet instead of gridlines. (See "Borders and Lines" in the section "Formatting.")

(See also "Hiding: Gridlines" in the section "Customizing.")

Publishing to the Web

Excel now enables you to publish your existing worksheet data and charts to the World Wide Web. You can use the Internet Assistant from within Excel to create an HTML-based Web page from your worksheet data or charts. If you want to collect information from those who visit your Web site, you can also set up an Excel form to compile the data. For additional information, search on "publishing data on the Internet" in Microsoft Excel Help.

Steps

1. Open the workbook, and then click a cell within the data range that you want to convert to a Web page.

2. Choose File, Save As HTML. The Internet Assistant Wizard appears.

3. Follow the instructions provided in the Internet Assistant Wizard.

NOTE   If the Save As HTML command doesn't appear on the File menu, you need to install the Internet Assistant add-in program. Choose Tools, Add-Ins, then select Internet Assistant Wizard and click OK. If the Internet Assistant Wizard doesn't appear in the Add-Ins Available list, you may want to install the Wizard from the Excel 97 or Office 97 CD. ■

(See also "Internet: Browsing Web Pages" and "Internet: Creating Hyperlinks" in the section "File Management.")

Sending E-Mail from Excel

If you want several people to receive a copy of your workbook at the same time, you can send a workbook to them as electronic mail from within Excel. (See "Shared Workbooks: Setting Up" in the section "File Management," if you want to route a workbook to a group of people, one person at a time.)

To send Excel workbooks through electronic mail, you need to use either Microsoft Exchange (or another mail system compatible with MAPI) or Lotus cc:Mail (or another mail system compatible with VIM). For additional information, search on "electronic mail" in Microsoft Excel Help.

NOTE To perform this procedure, you must have already installed electronic mail software and hardware. ■

Steps

1. Your e-mail program must be open and running. Open the workbook that you want to distribute via electronic mail and choose File, Send To, Mail Recipient.

2. If a Mail Login dialog box appears, fill in the data requested and click OK. The New Message dialog box appears; click the Address button.

3. The Address Message dialog box appears. Type the information requested, and then click Done.

4. Click in the text box of the New Message window and type your message. To send an Excel file or any other file along with the message, click the Attach button and navigate the folders in the Message Item Attachment dialog box until you find the worksheet or other file you want to send. Select the file, and then click Attach.

5. The New Message dialog box appears again. Select the Priority of the mail (Low, Normal, or Urgent) and whether you want to be notified when the message has been received by the recipient(s). Click Send to complete the mailing.

NOTE Depending on the e-mail system you are using, your messages may be sent immediately or on a scheduled basis. Many e-mail systems have a feature called an outbox, a send out folder, or something similar where you can check to see whether the message has been sent. Check with your e-mail administrator (if applicable) to better understand the mailing timing and the verification methods for your particular e-mail system. ■

Functions Mini-Reference

This section is a reference of the more commonly used Excel functions from the following function categories: Database, Date and Time, Financial, Information, Logical, Lookup and Reference, Math and Trigonometry, Statistical, and Text. Refer to the section titled "Formula & Function Management," earlier in this book, for general information on entering and using functions.

Each of the following subsections begins with a brief description of the function category, followed by information on specific functions in that category. Information supplied on these functions includes the syntax, a description of the function, what you need to supply for the function to work, what the resulting information will be, and examples (for selected functions), as well as occasional tips, notes, cautions, and troubleshooting items.

Because Microsoft does not provide paper documentation of Excel's functions, we have included the most common and useful functions in this convenient reference. For information on some of the less used functions, or additional information on the more complex aspects of these functions, choose Help, Contents and Index (in Excel). Then click the Index tab and search on "functions."

NOTE Function arguments appear in *italic* throughout this section. In syntax lines, all required arguments are indicated in ***bold italic***; optional arguments appear in *italic* only. ■

Database Functions

The database functions provide summary statistics on a database or list in a worksheet. They enable you to analyze whether values in the list meet a specified condition, or *criteria*. Excel's database functions all use the same arguments: *database, field,* and *criteria*. These arguments can represent any range you specify in the worksheet.

For the *database* argument in any database function, you can specify a cell range (such as A5:G20) or a range name (such as DATABASE). Be sure to include the headers row in the *database* range or range name.

The *field* argument indicates the column you want to average. You can specify the field by its field name in quotation marks (such as "City"), by a reference to the cell containing the field name (such as E5), or by a number—1 always represents the first field (or column) in the database, 2 is the second, and so on.

The *criteria* argument can be a cell range (such as A1:G3), or a range name (such as CRITERIA). The criteria you enter in a worksheet must not overlap the database. Also, do not place the criteria range below the database, or it may be overwritten as you add records to the database.

Database Average

Syntax: =DAVERAGE (*database, field, criteria*) The DAVERAGE function averages the numbers in the *field* of the *database* for those records that satisfy the *criteria*.

You Supply: *database* as the cell range or range name of the entire list; *field* as the field name in quotation marks, the cell reference of the field name, or the position of the field number in the database (use 1 for the first field, 2 for the second, and so on); *criteria* as a cell range or a range name.

Result is: the average of the numbers in the column of the list that match the criteria you specify.

Example: In the following formula, the *database* being ana-
lyzed resides in B10:G75, the *field* being averaged has the
heading Items, and the *criteria* is in a range with the name
CritSales. Remember to use quotation marks when you reference a specific field name.

```
=DAVERAGE(B10:G75,"Items",CritSales)
```

Database Count (Nonblank Cells)

Syntax: =DCOUNTA (*database,field,criteria*) The
DCOUNTA function counts the number of nonblank cells in
the *field* of the *database* for those records that satisfy the criteria. If the field argument is omitted, DCOUNTA counts all
nonblank records in the *database* that satisfy the criteria.

You Supply: *database* as the cell range or range name of the
entire list; (optional) *field* as the field name in quotation marks,
the cell reference of the field name, or the position of the field
number in the database (use 1 for the first field, 2 for the second, and so on); *criteria* as a cell range or a range name.

Result is: the total count of the nonblank cells in the column
of the list that match the criteria you specify.

Database Count (Numeric Cells)

Syntax: =DCOUNT (*database,field,criteria*) The
DCOUNT function counts the cells containing numbers in the
field of the *database* for those records that satisfy the *criteria*.
If the *field* argument is omitted, DCOUNT counts all records
in the *database* that satisfy the *criteria*.

You Supply: *database* as the cell range or range name of the
entire list; (optional) *field* as the field name in quotation marks,
the cell reference of the field name, or the position of the field
number in the database (use 1 for the first field, 2 for the second, and so on); *criteria* as a cell range or a range name.

Result is: the total count of the cells with numbers in the column of the list that match the criteria you specify.

Database Get Record

Syntax: =DGET (*database,field,criteria*) The DGET
function extracts from the *database* the single record that

matches the *criteria*. If no records match the *criteria*, #VALUE! is returned. If more than one record matches the *criteria*, #NUM! is returned.

You Supply: *database* as the cell range or range name of the entire list; *field* as the field name in quotation marks, the cell reference of the field name, or the position of the field number in the database (use 1 for the first field, 2 for the second, and so on); *criteria* as a cell range or a range name.

Result is: the record that matches the criteria you specify (or #VALUE! if no records match, or #NUM! if more than one record matches).

Database Maximum
Syntax: **=DMAX (*database,field,criteria*)**   The DMAX function finds the largest number in the *field* of the *database* for records that satisfy the *criteria*.

You Supply: *database* as the cell range or range name of the entire list; *field* as the field name in quotation marks, the cell reference of the field name, or the field number in the database (use 1 for the first field, 2 for the second, and so on); *criteria* as a cell range or a range name.

Result is: the maximum value in the column of the list that matches the criteria you specify.

Database Minimum
Syntax: **=DMIN (*database,field,criteria*)**   The DMIN function finds the smallest number in the *field* of the *database* for records that satisfy the *criteria*.

You Supply: *database* as the cell range or range name of the entire list; *field* as the field name in quotation marks, the cell reference of the field name, or the position of the field number in the database (use 1 for the first field, 2 for the second, and so on); *criteria* as a cell range or a range name.

Result is: the minimum value in the column of the list that matches the criteria you specify.

Database Product

Syntax: **=DPRODUCT(*database,field,criteria*)** The DPRODUCT function multiplies all values in the *field* of the *database* for records that satisfy the *criteria*. This function is similar to DSUM, but the values are multiplied rather than added.

You Supply: *database* as the cell range or range name of the entire list; *field* as the field name in quotation marks, the cell reference of the field name, or the position of the field number in the database (use 1 for the first field, 2 for the second, and so on); *criteria* as a cell range or a range name.

Result is: the product of all values in the column of the list that match the criteria you specify.

Database Standard Deviation (Entire Population)

Syntax: **=DSTDEVP (*database,field,criteria*)** The DSTDEVP function calculates the standard deviation of the entire population, based on the numbers in the *field* of the *database* for records that satisfy the *criteria*.

You Supply: *database* as the cell range or range name of the entire list; *field* as the field name in quotation marks, the cell reference of the field name, or the position of the field number in the database (use 1 for the first field, 2 for the second, and so on); *criteria* as a cell range or a range name.

Result is: the standard deviation of an entire population, based on the values in the column of the list that match the criteria you specify.

Database Standard Deviation (Sample Population)

Syntax: **=DSTDEV (*database,field,criteria*)** The DSTDEV function calculates the standard deviation of a sample population, based on the numbers in the *field* of the *database* for records that satisfy the *criteria*.

You Supply: *database* as the cell range or range name of the entire list; *field* as the field name in quotation marks, the cell reference of the field name, or the position of the field number in the database (use 1 for the first field, 2 for the second, and so on); *criteria* as a cell range or a range name.

Result is: the standard deviation of a sample population, based on the values in the column of the list that match the criteria you specify.

Database Sum

Syntax: =DSUM (*database,field,criteria*)   The DSUM function totals all numbers in the *field* of the *database* for records that satisfy the *criteria*.

You Supply: *database* as the cell range or range name of the entire list; *field* as the field name in quotation marks, the cell reference of the field name, or the position of the field number in the database (use 1 for the first field, 2 for the second, and so on); *criteria* as a cell range or a range name.

Result is: the sum of all values in the column of the list that match the criteria you specify.

Database Variance (Entire Population)

Syntax: =DVARP (*database,field,criteria*)   The DVARP function calculates the variance of an entire population, based on the numbers in the *field* of the *database* for records that satisfy the *criteria*.

You Supply: *database* as the cell range or range name of the entire list; *field* as the field name in quotation marks, the cell reference of the field name, or the position of the field number in the database (use 1 for the first field, 2 for the second, and so on); *criteria* as a cell range or a range name.

Result is: the estimated variance of an entire population, based on the values in the column of the list that match the criteria you specify.

Database Variance (Sample Population)

Syntax: =DVAR (*database,field,criteria*)   The DVAR function calculates the estimated variance (how the sample deviates from the average) of a sample population, based on the numbers in the *field* of the *database* for records that satisfy the *criteria*.

You Supply: *database* as the cell range or range name of the entire list; *field* as the field name in quotation marks, the cell reference of the field name, or the position of the field number in the database (use 1 for the first field, 2 for the second, and so on); *criteria* as a cell range or a range name.

Result is: the estimated variance of a sample population, based on the values in the column of the list that match the criteria you specify.

Date and Time Functions

Although Excel can display dates and times in many different formats, Excel actually stores all dates as *serial numbers* and all times as fractions. The serial number represents the number of days from January 1, 1900, until the date you specify; a time is a decimal fraction of 24 hours. Serial numbers enable you to more easily perform calculations on dates, such as the number of days between two dates. The serial number for July 1, 1997, 3:00 p.m., is 35612.625, where 35612 is the number of days from the beginning of the century and .625 is the decimal fraction of 24 hours representing 3:00 p.m.

NOTE When a date or time function includes the *serial_number* argument, you can supply a serial date number or a reference to a cell containing a date or time. ■

Date Serial Number
Syntax: **=DATE (*year,month,day*)** The DATE function produces the *serial number* for a specific date. Use DATE to calculate a serial number in formulas that produce a numeric year, month, or day. For example, you can use this function to determine the amount of days an account is past due by calculating the difference between the serial numbers of the date due and the current date.

FUNCTIONS MINI-REFERENCE

TIP   Use the formula **=DATE** (*year,month*+1,0) to calculate the last day of the specified *month*. For example, **=DATE** (97,11+1,0) returns 11/30/97.

You Supply: *year* as a number from 1900 to 9999, or a reference to a cell containing a year number; *month* as a number from 1 to 12, or a reference to a cell containing a month number; and *day* as a number from 1 to 31, or a reference to a cell containing a day number.

Result is: a serial number that represents the specified date. If Excel displays the result in a Date format, change the cell format to General to see the serial number.

Example: The following formula produces the serial number 35612 if cell C20 contains the day number 1:

```
=DATE(1997,7,C20)
```

Day Serial Number

Syntax: =DAY(*serial_number*)   The DAY function converts a *serial_number* to the number of the day of the month between 1 and 31. Format the cell as a number.

You Supply: *serial_number* as a number between 0 and 2958465, or as a date format that Excel recognizes.

Result is: a number representing the day of the month, between 1 and 31. If Excel displays the result in a Date format, change the cell format to General to see the serial number.

Examples: Each of the following formulas produce the day number 16:

```
=DAY(35627)
```
```
=DAY("16-Jul-97")
```

Hour Serial Number

Syntax: =HOUR(*serial_number*)   Hours are included in the fractional part of a day in a serial number. The HOUR function returns the hour number (based on a 24-hour clock) for the fractional day in the *serial_number.* Format the cell as a number.

You Supply: *serial_number* as a number between 0 and 2958465, or as a time format that Excel recognizes.

Result is: a number representing the hour of the day, between 0 (12:00 a.m.) and 23 (11:00 p.m.). If Excel displays the result in a Time format, change the cell format to General to see the serial number.

Example: The following formula produces the hour number 18:

```
=HOUR(35627.75)
```

Minute Serial Number

Syntax: **=MINUTE(*serial_number*)** The MINUTE function returns the number of minutes from a *serial_number*. The fractional part of a day is based on a 24-hour clock. Format the cell as a number.

You Supply: *serial_number* as a number between 0 and 2958465, or as a time format that Excel recognizes.

Result is: a number representing the minute of the hour, between 0 and 59. If Excel displays the result in a Time format, change the cell format to General to see the serial number.

Example: The following formula produces the minute number 7:

```
=MINUTE(35627.755)
```

Month Serial Number

Syntax: **=MONTH(*serial_number*)** The MONTH function converts the *serial_number* to the number of the month (from 1 to 12). Format the cell as a number.

You Supply: *serial_number* as a number between 0 and 2958465, or as a date format that Excel recognizes.

Result is: a number representing the month of the year, between 1 and 12. If Excel displays the result in a Date format, change the cell format to General to see the serial number.

Example: The following formula produces the month number 7:

```
=MONTH(35627)
```

Now (Current Date and Time)

Syntax: =NOW( ) The NOW function calculates the serial number of the date and time in the computer's clock. Excel updates the date and time only when the worksheet is opened or recalculated. Be sure to include the empty parentheses when entering this function. NOW does not use an argument.

Use the NOW function to stamp a worksheet with the date and time. Type =NOW( ) in a cell. If the result doesn't appear as a date and time, format the cell with the desired date or time format. (See also the "Today (Current Date)" function.)

TIP   To freeze a date or time you entered with the NOW function, copy the cell with Edit, Copy; then use Edit, Paste Special (with the Values option) to paste over the cell you copied.

You Supply: only the function name followed by empty parentheses. The NOW function uses no arguments.

Result is: the current date and time, in the format m/d/yy h:mm (such as 11/6/97 21:41).

Second Serial Number

Syntax: =SECOND(*serial_number*)

The SECOND function returns the number of seconds (between 0 and 59) in the fractional part of the *serial_number*.

You Supply: *serial_number* as a number between 0 and 2958465, or as a time format that Excel recognizes.

Result is: a number representing the second of the hour, between 0 and 59. If Excel displays the result in a Time format, change the cell format to General to see the serial number.

Time Serial Number

Syntax: =TIME(*hour,minute,second*) The TIME function calculates the serial number when given the *hour, minute,* and *second* of time on a 24-hour clock. The time format 0:00:00 represents 12:00:00 a.m., and the format 23:59:59 represents 11:59:59 p.m.

You Supply: *hour* as a number from 0 to 23, or a reference to a cell containing an hour number; *minute* as a number from 0 to 59, or a reference to a cell containing a minute number; and *second* as a number from 0 to 59, or a reference to a cell containing a second number.

Result is: a decimal number from 0 to 0.999988426 that represents the specified time. If Excel displays the result in a Time format, change the cell format to General to see the decimal number.

Example: The following formula produces the decimal number .903646 in the General format:

```
=TIME(21,41,15)
```

Today (Current Date)

Syntax: **=TODAY( )** The TODAY function calculates the serial number of the computer's current date. This acts the same as the NOW function, but does not return the decimal (time) portion of the serial number. Excel updates the serial number when the worksheet is opened or recalculated.

Use the TODAY function to stamp a worksheet with the current date. Type **=TODAY( )** in a cell. If the result doesn't appear as a date, format the cell with the desired date format. (See also the "Now (Current Date and Time)" function.)

TIP To freeze the date you entered with the TODAY function, copy the cell with Edit, Copy; then use Edit, Paste Special (with the Values option) to paste over the cell you copied.

You Supply: only the function name followed by empty parentheses. The TODAY function uses no arguments.

Result is: the current date, in the format m/d/yy (such as 11/6/97).

Weekday Serial Number

Syntax: **=WEEKDAY(*serial_number*,*return_type*)** The WEEKDAY function converts the *serial_number* to the day of the week. The result is a number from 1 (Sunday) to 7 (Saturday). The optional *return_type* argument determines what day of the week to start with. With a *return_type* of 1 (or no return type), number 1 is Sunday and 7 is Saturday. With a *return_type* of 2, number 1 is Monday and 7 is Sunday. With a *return_type* of 3, number 0 is Monday and 6 is Sunday.

You Supply: *serial_number* as a number between 0 and 2958465, or as a date format that Excel recognizes; (optional) *return_type* as a number between 1 and 3.

Result is: a number representing the number of the day of the week, from 1 to 7. If Excel displays the result in a Date format, change the cell format to General to see the serial number.

Example: The following formula produces 5 (Friday):

```
=WEEKDAY("4-Jul-97",2)
```

Year Serial Number

Syntax: **=YEAR(*serial_number*)** The YEAR function converts the *serial_number* into the year.

You Supply: *serial_number* as a number between 0 and 2958465, or as a date format that Excel recognizes.

Result is: a number representing the year, between 1900 and 9999. If Excel displays the result in a Date format, change the cell format to General to see the serial number.

Example: The following formula produces the year 1997:

```
=YEAR(35627)
```

Financial Functions

Instead of entering and calculating complex financial equations manually, you can use Excel's financial functions to greatly ease this task. Excel provides several financial functions that solve annuity problems. An annuity is a series of regular cash flows over a period of time. For example, cash flows may be housing payments that occur according to a regular time period.

Excel also includes financial functions to analyze uneven cash flows and to calculate depreciation using the double-declining balance depreciation method.

TROUBLESHOOTING **The error #NUM! appeared in the cell after I entered a financial function. What does this mean?**
You may have incorrectly entered the positive or negative signs for *pmt* or *pv*. Remember that money you are paying out should appear as a negative number.

Future Value

Syntax: **=FV(*rate,nper,pmt,pv,type*)** The FV function determines the future value of a series of cash flows of equal *pmt* amounts made at even periods for *nper* periods at the constant interest *rate*. A lump sum, *pv*, can be invested at the beginning of the term. If no values are entered for *pv* and *type*, they are considered to be zero. The periodic interest (*rate*) must have the same unit as *nper*—the number of periods (such as months) in the life of the cash flow. For example, the annual interest rate should be divided by 12 if payments or receipts are monthly.

You Supply: *rate* as the interest rate per period; *nper* as the total number of periods; *pmt* as the payment amount made each period; (optional) *pv* as the present value; (optional) *type* as 0 if payment is at the end of the period, or 1 if payment is at the beginning of the period.

Result is: the future value of the investment, expressed in a dollar amount.

Example: The following formula calculates the worth of an investment at the end of the term, if you invest $1,000 as a lump sum and add $200 at the start of each month for 5 years (60 months) at an interest rate of 8 percent compounded monthly:

```
=FV(.08/12,60,-200,-1000,1)
```

The result is $16,283.19. Notice that amounts you pay out are expressed using negative numbers.

FUNCTIONS MINI-REFERENCE

Interest Portion of a Payment

Syntax: =IPMT(*rate,per,nper,pv,fv,type*)   The IPMT function calculates the interest portion of a payment on an annuity. You can use this function to calculate the interest paid on a mortgage at some period, *per,* within the term of the mortgage, *nper.* The value of *per* must be in the range 1 to *nper.* If no values are entered for *fv* and *type,* they are considered to be zero.

You Supply: *rate* as the interest rate per period; *per* as the period number; *nper* as the total number of periods; *pv* as the present value; (optional) *fv* as the future value; (optional) *type* as 0 if payment is at the end of the period, or 1 if payment is at the beginning of the period.

Result is: the interest payment for the specified period, expressed in a dollar amount.

Example: The following formula calculates how much was paid toward interest in the tenth month for a flat-rate mortgage of $130,000 made at 9 percent interest for 20 years:

```
=IPMT(.09/12,10,240,130000)
```

The result is ($961.46). The result is negative because it is the amount you paid out.

Interest Rate

Syntax: =RATE(*nper,pmt,pv,fv,type,guess*)   The RATE function calculates the interest rate for the annuity that you define with the arguments. If no values are entered for *fv* and *type,* they are considered to be zero. If you do not enter an estimated interest rate for *guess,* Excel uses 10 percent (.1). RATE can return more than one solution, depending on the value used for *guess.* If *guess* is too far from the correct value, Excel may not be able to make an estimate and may return #NUM!.

You Supply: *nper* as the total number of periods; *pmt* as the payment amount; *pv* as the present value; (optional) *fv* as the future value; (optional) *type* as 0 if payment is at the end of the period, or 1 if payment is at the beginning of the period; (optional) *guess* as your guess for what the rate will be.

Result is: the interest rate per period, expressed as a percentage.

Example: The following formula results in an interest rate of 1.02 percent per month:

```
=RATE(36,-400,12000)
```

Net Present Value

(e)Syntax: =NPV(*rate,value1,value2, ...*)   The NPV function calculates the net present value of a series of cash flows found in the range or array of *value1, value2,* and so on, given a discount rate equal to *rate.* The net present value of a series of cash flows is the value that a future stream of cash represents in terms of cash today, given the fact that future cash can be invested to earn the *rate* percentage. The cash flows are considered to be at the end of each period. Cash flows do not have to be equal amounts. The *rate* is the rate per period.

You Supply: *rate* as the discount rate per period; *value1* as the first cash flow; (optional) *value2* as the second cash flow; and so on up to 29 maximum cash flow amounts.

Result is: the net present value, expressed in a dollar amount.

Number of Periods

Syntax: =NPER(*rate,pmt,pv,fv,type*)   The NPER function calculates the number of periods required to create the annuity specified by the given arguments. If no values are entered for *fv* and *type,* they are considered to be zero.

You Supply: *rate* as the interest rate per period; *pmt* as the payment amount made each period; *pv* as the present value; (optional) *fv* as the future value; (optional) *type* as 0 if payment is at the end of the period, or 1 if payment is at the beginning of the period.

Result is: the number of periods for an investment.

Example: The following formula calculates the number of periods required for an annuity totaling $10,000, with payments of $500 per period at 10 percent interest.

```
=NPER(0.10/12,-500,10000)
```

The result is approximately 22 payments.

Periodic Payment

Syntax: =PMT(*rate,nper,pv,fv,type*) The PMT function calculates the periodic payment for different *types* and future values (*fv*) of investments given the investment's *rate*, term (*nper*), and present value (*pv*). If no values are entered for *fv* and *type*, they are considered to be zero.

You Supply: *rate* as the interest rate per period; *nper* as the total number of periods; *pv* as the present value; (optional) *fv* as the future value; (optional) *type* as 0 if payment is at the end of the period, or 1 if payment is at the beginning of the period.

Result is: the periodic payment for a loan, expressed in a dollar amount.

Example: The following formula calculates the periodic payment for a loan totaling $120,000 over 30 years at 10 percent interest:

```
=PMT(.1/12,360,120000)
```

The result is ($1,053.09). The result is negative because it represents the amount you pay out.

Present Value

Syntax: =PV(*rate,nper,pmt,fv,type*) The PV function calculates the present value of a series of future cash flows of equal *pmt* amounts made at even periods for *nper* periods at the constant interest *rate*. PV is the amount in current dollars that equals an even cash flow in the future. If the amounts of the cash flow are uneven, use the NPV function. If no values are entered for *fv* and *type*, they are considered to be zero.

You Supply: *rate* as the interest rate per period; *nper* as the total number of periods; *pmt* as the payment amount;

(optional) *fv* as the future value; (optional) *type* as 0 if payment is at the end of the period, or 1 if payment is at the beginning of the period.

Result is: the present value of an investment (the total amount a series of future payments is worth now), expressed in a dollar amount.

Example: The following formula calculates the total amount of a car loan you can afford if you know that you can pay $300 per month for the next four years at 11 percent interest:

```
=PV(0.11/12,48,-300)
```

The result is $11,607.43.

Principal Portion of a Payment

Syntax: **=PPMT(*rate,per,nper,pv,fv,type*)** The PPMT function calculates the principal portion of a payment made on an amortized investment. This portion is the part of the PMT function that reduces a loan balance. If no values are entered for *fv* and *type,* they are considered to be zero.

You Supply: *rate* as the interest rate per period; *per* as the period number; *nper* as the total number of periods; *pv* as the present value; (optional) *fv* as the future value; (optional) *type* as 0 if payment is at the end of the period, or 1 if payment is at the beginning of the period.

Result is: the principal portion of a payment for the specified period, expressed in a dollar amount.

Example: The following formula calculates how much was paid toward principal in the tenth month for a flat-rate mortgage of $130,000 made at 9 percent interest for 20 years:

```
=PPMT(.09/12,10,240,130000)
```

The result is ($208.18). The result is negative because it is the amount you paid out.

Straight-Line Depreciation

Syntax: **=SLN(*cost,salvage,life*)** The SLN function returns the annual amount of straight-line depreciation when given the initial *cost* of an item, the *salvage* value at the end of the item's economic life, and the economic *life* of the item.

You Supply: *cost* as the initial cost of the asset; *salvage* as the salvage value at the end of the life of the asset; *life* as the useful life of the asset.

Result is: the straight-line depreciation of an asset for one period, expressed as a dollar amount.

Example: The following formula results in depreciation of $900 per year:

```
=SLN(12000,7500,5)
```

Sum-of-Years' Digits Depreciation

Syntax: =SYD(*cost,salvage,life,per*) The SYD function calculates the depreciation for the period, *per,* using the sum-of-years' digits depreciation method. You must indicate the initial *cost,* the *salvage* value at the end of the economic life, and the *life* of the item.

You Supply: *cost* as the initial cost of the asset; *salvage* as the salvage value at the end of the life of the asset; *life* as the useful life of the asset; *per* as the period.

Result is: the sum-of-years' digits depreciation of an asset for a specified period, expressed as a dollar amount.

Examples: The following formulas result in depreciation of $1,500 for the first year, and $1,200 for the second year for the same asset:

```
=SYD(12000,7500,5,1)
=SYD(12000,7500,5,2)
```

Variable-Declining Balance Depreciation

Syntax: =VDB(*cost,salvage,life,start_ period, end_ period,factor,no_switch*) The variable-declining balance depreciation function returns the depreciation on an asset for the period you indicate. The *cost, salvage,* and *life* arguments have the same definitions as described in earlier functions.

Start_period is the period at which you want to start calculating depreciation and *end_period* is the ending period for the calculation. Both must be in the same units as the *life*. *Factor* is the rate at which the balance declines. If *factor* is omitted, it is assumed to be 2 (for double-declining balance).

No_switch is a logical argument indicating whether VDB should switch to straight-line depreciation when it is greater than the declining-balance depreciation. Using TRUE for *no_switch* prevents the switch to straight-line method. FALSE, or omitting the *no_switch* argument, switches to the straight-line method. All arguments must be positive.

You Supply: *cost* as the initial cost of the asset; *salvage* as the salvage value at the end of the life of the asset; *life* as the useful life of the asset; *start_period* as the period to start calculating depreciation; *end_period* as the ending period for the calculation; (optional) *factor* as the rate at which the balance declines; (optional) *no_switch* as TRUE to prevent switching to SLD, or FALSE to switch to SLD.

Result is: the variable-declining balance depreciation of an asset for a specified period, expressed in a dollar amount.

Information Functions

The information functions are provided primarily for compatibility with worksheets from other vendors. These functions enable you to test for conditions such as which worksheets are open, whether a cell is formatted with Times Roman italic, whether the worksheet is running on a Mac or PC, and how much memory is available.

Environment Information

Syntax: **=INFO(*type_text*)**   The INFO function returns information on the current operating environment. Use the *type_text* argument to indicate what type of information you want. The following table lists specific arguments you can use for *type_text*.

FUNCTIONS MINI-REFERENCE

Arguments Used for *type_text*

Type_text	Returned Value
"directory"	Current directory
"memavail"	Memory available
"memused"	Memory used for data, in bytes
"numfile"	Number of active worksheets
"origin"	Absolute A1-style of references as text
"osversion"	Operating system version
"recalc"	Recalculation mode: Automatic or Manual
"release"	Microsoft Excel version
"system"	Operating system name: Windows = pcdos; Macintosh = Mac
"totmem"	Memory available, in bytes; includes memory in use

You Supply: *type_text* as text in quotation marks that specifies the type of information you want on the current operating environment.

Result is: the returned value, based on the *type_text* argument you specify (refer to table above).

Example: The following formula returns Automatic if your worksheet is set to automatic calculation:

```
=INFO("recalc")
```

IS (Condition) Functions

Syntax: =**ISfunction(*value*)** Excel provides 11 functions that determine whether a cell meets certain conditions, such as whether it is blank or contains an error value. Depending on the status of the cell, the IS*function* produces either a TRUE or FALSE *value*. IS*functions* are most useful when used with the IF function to test whether a cell or range is blank or contains numbers, text, or errors. You also can use IS*functions* to test for the appropriate type of entry. The IS*functions* and their results are listed in the following table.

IS Functions and Results Returned

Function	Result
ISBLANK(*value*)	TRUE if value is a blank reference; FALSE if value is nonblank
ISERR(*value*)	TRUE if value is any error other than #N/A; FALSE for any other value
ISERROR(*value*)	TRUE if value is any error value; FALSE if value is not an error value
ISEVEN(*value*)	TRUE if the integer portion of the value is an even number; FALSE if the value is odd
ISLOGICAL(*value*)	TRUE if value is a logical value; FALSE if value is not a logical value
ISNA(*value*)	TRUE if value is the #N/A error value; FALSE if value is not #N/A
ISNONTEXT(*value*)	TRUE if value is not text; FALSE if value is text
ISNUMBER(*value*)	TRUE if value is a number; FALSE if value is not a number
ISODD(*value*)	TRUE if the integer portion of the value is an odd number; FALSE if the value is even
ISREF(*value*)	TRUE if value is a reference; FALSE if value is not a reference
ISTEXT(*value*)	TRUE if value is text; FALSE if value is not text

You Supply: *value* as the value you want to test; *value* can refer to a cell, name, or formula.

Result is: TRUE or FALSE, depending on the result of the test.

Example: The following formula includes an IF function to test whether or not cell C10 contains a number. If cell C10 contains a number, then the cell containing the formula displays Valid entry; otherwise the cell displays Please enter a number. (See also the "Logical IF" function.)

```
=IF(ISNUMBER(C10),"Valid entry","Please enter
a number")
```

No Value Available

Syntax: =NA( ) The NA function always produces the error value #N/A, which means "No value available." NA does not use an argument, but the parentheses are required. You can type **#N/A** directly into a cell to obtain the same result. Use this function to mark empty cells in the worksheet and avoid unintentionally including blank cells in your calculations. If you enter **#N/A** into blank data-entry cells, for example, the formulas that depend on those cells result in #N/A.

You Supply: only the function name followed by empty parentheses. The NA function uses no arguments.

Result is: the value #N/A.

Type of Cell Contents

Syntax: =TYPE(*value*) The TYPE function determines the type of a cell's contents and produces a corresponding code, as shown in the table below.

Cell Contents Code for the TYPE Function

Value	Result
Number	1
Text	2
Logical value	4

Value	Result
Formula	8
Error value	16
Array	64

You Supply: *value* as a value, cell reference, or formula.

Result is: either 1, 2, 4, 8, 16, or 64, depending on the type of cell contents (see table above).

Example: The following formula results in 1 if cell J24 contains a number; if cell J24 contains text, the formula result is 2:

```
=TYPE(J24)
```

Logical Functions

The logical functions enable you to add decision-making and logical tests to your worksheets. The IF statement is useful for testing conditions and making decisions based on a cell's contents. The AND and OR functions can test multiple criteria or test conditions for use in IF functions.

Logical AND

Syntax: =AND(*logical1,logical2, ...*) The AND function joins test conditions, and returns TRUE if all *logical* arguments are TRUE; or FALSE if any *logical* argument is FALSE. Arguments for the AND function must be single logical values (or arrays that contain logical values) and they cannot contain more than 30 logical values. The #VALUE! error appears if there are no logical values in the arguments.

You Supply: *logical1* as the first condition you want to test; (optional) *logical2* as the second condition you want to test; and so on up to 30 conditions maximum.

Result is: TRUE if all *logical* arguments are TRUE; or FALSE if any one *logical* argument is FALSE.

Example: The following formula result is TRUE only when D15 is not zero and G23 is less than 30:

```
=AND(D15,G23<30)
```

Logical FALSE

Syntax: **=FALSE( )** The FALSE function always produces a logical FALSE result and uses no arguments. You can type the FALSE function with or without the parentheses.

You Supply: only the function name, or the function name followed by empty parentheses. The FALSE function uses no arguments.

Result is: always FALSE.

Logical IF

Syntax: **=IF(*logical_test,value_if_true,value_if_false*)** The IF function produces *value_if_true* when the *logical_test* evaluates as TRUE; or produces *value_if_false* when the *logical_test* evaluates as FALSE. If *value_if_true* is omitted, Excel returns the value TRUE when *logical_test* evaluates as TRUE. If *value_if_false* is omitted, Excel returns the value FALSE when *logical_test* evaluates as FALSE. IF is one of the most valuable functions in Excel; this function can test cells and make decisions based on the cell contents. Use the AND, OR, and NOT as the *logical_test* function with the IF function to make complex decisions.

You Supply: *logical_test* as any value or expression that can evaluate to TRUE or FALSE; (optional) *value_if_true* as the value that is returned if *logical_test* is TRUE; and (optional) *value_if_false* as the value that is returned if *logical_test* is FALSE. Use quotation marks for *value_if_true* or *value_if_false* if the argument is to return the specified text.

Result is: the *value_if_true* argument if the test evaluates to TRUE, or the *value_if_false* argument if the test evaluates to FALSE.

Example: The following formula returns Valid if the contents of cell D17 is greater than 10 and less than 30; otherwise the formula returns Invalid:

```
=IF(AND(D17>10,D17<30),"Valid","Invalid")
```

Logical NOT

Syntax: =NOT(*logical*) The NOT function reverses the result of the *logical* argument from TRUE to FALSE or from FALSE to TRUE. Use this function to return the opposite condition of the *logical_test* in an IF statement.

You Supply: *logical* as any value or expression that can evaluate to TRUE or FALSE.

Result is: FALSE for a TRUE result, or TRUE for a FALSE result.

Example: The following formula tests whether cell D17 contains the result 10 or 30 and produces the message Not 10 or 30 when the cell does not contain either of those results; otherwise, the formula result is Contains 10 or 30:

```
=IF(NOT(OR(D17=10,D17=30)),"Not 10 or 30","Contains
10 or 30")
```

Logical OR

Syntax: =OR(*logical1*,*logical2*,...) The OR function joins test conditions, and returns TRUE if one or more logical arguments is TRUE; or FALSE only when all logical arguments are FALSE. OR is limited to 30 or fewer arguments. Arguments cannot be blank cells, error values, or text.

TIP Use IS*functions* within OR functions to test for blank cells, error values, or text.

You Supply: *logical1* as the first condition you want to test; (optional) *logical2* as the second condition you want to test; and so on up to 30 conditions maximum.

Result is: TRUE if any *logical* argument is TRUE; or FALSE if all *logical* arguments are FALSE.

Example: The following formula tests whether cell D17 contains the result 10 or 30 and produces the message Contains

10 or 30 when it does; otherwise, the formula produces the message Not 10 or 30:

```
=IF(OR(D17=10,D17=30),"Contains 10 or 30","Not 10
or 30")
```

Logical TRUE

Syntax: =TRUE( )   The TRUE function always produces a logical TRUE result, and uses no arguments. You can type the TRUE argument with or without the parentheses.

You Supply: only the function name, or the function name followed by empty parentheses. The TRUE function uses no arguments.

Result is: always TRUE.

Lookup and Reference Functions

The lookup functions enable your worksheets to retrieve a value from within a table. You can use the INDEX function, for example, to extract specific values from within an array. The reference functions are necessary when you need to determine cell contents, ranges, or selected areas. Some of them, such as OFFSET, also are used in macro sheets.

Address in Text Form

Syntax: =ADDRESS(*row_num,column_num,abs_num, a1,sheet_text*)   The ADDRESS function produces a cell reference in text form for the cell indicated by the *row_num* and *col_num*. Use one of four values in *abs_num* to specify the type of reference: absolute reference (the default) is 1; absolute row, relative column is 2; relative row, absolute column is 3; and relative reference is 4.

If the *a1* argument is TRUE, or omitted, Excel returns A1 style cell references. FALSE returns the R1C1 style cell reference. The *sheet_text* argument is the name of the worksheet or macro sheet used by the reference.

You Supply: *row_num* as the row number for the cell reference; *column_num* as the column number for the cell reference;

(optional) *abs_num* as the reference type; (optional) *a1* as a logical value that specifies the reference style; and (optional) *sheet_text* as the name of the worksheet to be used as the external reference.

Result is: a cell reference in text form for the cell indicated by the row number and column number you specify.

Example: The following formula returns $B17:

```
=ADDRESS(17,2,3,TRUE)
```

Areas Referenced

Syntax: =**AREAS(*reference*)** The AREAS function returns the number of areas in *reference*. Use the AREAS function to find how many selections are within an area.

You Supply: *reference* as a reference to one or more cells or ranges.

Result is: the number of areas in *reference*. Each area can be either a single cell or a range of cells.

Example: The following formula returns 2 when the range named PRINTAREA is defined as two separate ranges:

```
=AREAS(PRINTAREA)
```

Choose Value

Syntax: =**CHOOSE(*index_num,value1,value2, ...*)** The CHOOSE function selects from the list of *values* a value that corresponds to the *index_num*. For example, when the *index_num* is 2, the function chooses *value2*. CHOOSE displays #VALUE when the *index_num* is less than one or greater than the number of items in the list.

You Supply: *index_num* as a number between 1 and 29, specifying which value argument is selected; *value1* as a cell reference, name, formula, function, or text argument; (optional) *value2* as a cell reference, name, formula, function, or text argument; and so on up to 29 values maximum.

Result is: the value or action to perform from a list of values, based on the *index_num*.

FUNCTIONS MINI-REFERENCE

Example: The following formula returns 27 when cell A10 contains 4:

```
=CHOOSE(A10,21,7,19,27)
```

Column Number

Syntax: =COLUMN(*reference*) The COLUMN function produces the column number of the *reference* cell. If *reference* is an array or a range, then the column numbers of each column in the range return as a horizontal array. If the *reference* argument is not specified, COLUMN produces the column number of the cell that contains the function. *Reference* cannot contain multiple areas.

TIP Use the INDEX function instead of the COLUMN function if you want to read values from an array.

You Supply: *reference* as a cell reference or range.

Result is: the column number of the cell reference, or an array if *reference* is a range.

Horizontal Lookup

Syntax: =HLOOKUP(*lookup_value,table_array, row_index_num,range_lookup*) The HLOOKUP function looks across the top row of the range defined by *table_array* until the *lookup_value* is met; then looks down that column to the row specified by *row_index_num*. *Range_lookup* is a logical value (TRUE or FALSE). If the value is TRUE or omitted, HLOOKUP will return an approximate match. If FALSE, HLOOKUP will return an exact match or #N/A if no match is found.

Values in the first row of *table_array* must be in ascending order, both alphabetically (A - Z) and numerically (0 - 9). The *lookup_value* and the values in the first row of the *table_array* can be text, numbers, or logical values.

row_index_num begins with 1. To return a value from the first row, use 1, and from the second row, use 2, and so on. If *row_index_num* is less than 1, HLOOKUP produces the

#VALUE! error. If *row_index_num* is greater than the number of rows in the table, #REF! is displayed.

You Supply: *lookup_value* as a value, reference, or text string from the first row of the table; *table_array* as a reference to the table range; *row_index_num* as the row number in the table for the value you are looking up; and (optional) *range_lookup* as a logical value of TRUE or FALSE.

Result is: the value in the same column as *lookup_value* in a table, based on the row you specify; or #N/A if no match is found.

Hyperlink

Syntax: =HYPERLINK(*link_location, friendly_name*) The HYPERLINK function inserts a *hyperlink* into your worksheet that jumps to a specified linked location, such as a file on a hard drive or network, or an Internet address. The *link_location* argument is the full path and filename or the URL for an Internet address. The *friendly_name* argument is the text or value actually displayed in the cell. If you do not include a *friendly_name* argument the value of the *link_location* argument displays.

You Supply: *link_location* as the path and filename to a file, or a URL address; and (optional) *friendly_name* as the text you want to display in the cell (in place of the path and filename). Use quotation marks with the *friendly_name* argument.

Result is: the hyperlink, inserted in the current cell of the worksheet. Click the hyperlink to jump to the specified file or Internet address. You must have Internet access to use a hyperlink that jumps to an Internet address.

Index (Array)

Syntax: =INDEX(*array,row_num,column_num*) In the array form of the INDEX function, *row_num* and *column_num* return the value of a cell in the array. The definitions of *row_num* and *column_num* are the same as described in the reference version of the INDEX function.

FUNCTIONS MINI-REFERENCE

You Supply: *array* as a range of cells or array constant; *row_num* as the row from which to return a value; and (optional) *column_num* as the column from which to return a value.

Result is: a value or reference to a value in a table or range.

Example: The following formula returns 10:

```
=INDEX({2,3,4;10,11,12},2,1)
```

Index (Reference)

Syntax: **=INDEX(*reference*,*row_num*,*column_num*, *area_num*)** The reference form of the INDEX function produces a cell reference from within the *reference* specified, and at the intersection of the *row_num* and *column_num*. If *reference* is a single row or column, then either the *column_num* or *row_num* argument can be omitted (but not both). Other functions convert the value returned by INDEX to a cell reference or value as needed.

The referenced area is *reference*. If this area contains multiple ranges, enclose *reference* in parentheses with each range separated by commas. If *reference* contains more than one area, *area_num* can choose between areas. The arguments *row_num* and *column_num* choose a cell in the area specified. The first row or column is 1. Omitting the *row_num* or *column_num* or using 0 returns a reference for the entire row or column. A second form of the INDEX function is used with arrays.

NOTE If either *row_num* or *column_num* occurs outside the specified *reference* area, the INDEX function results in the message #REF! ■

You Supply: *reference* as a reference to one or more cell ranges; *row_num* as the row from which to return a value; (optional) *column_num* as the column from which to return a value; and (optional) *area_num* as a range in *reference* from which to return a value.

Result is: a value or reference to a value in a table or range.

Example: The following formula returns a reference or value in cell C5, which is the second row and third column in the first area:

```
=INDEX((A4:D7,F10:J15),2,3,1)
```

Lookup

Syntax: =**LOOKUP(***lookup_value,array***)** The array form of the LOOKUP function is similar to HLOOKUP and VLOOKUP. LOOKUP searches for a match to *lookup_value* in the first row or the first column of the *array*, depending on the shape of the *array*. If the *array* is square, or wider than tall, LOOKUP searches across the first row for the *lookup_value*. If the array is taller than it is wide, the search proceeds down the first column.

If LOOKUP cannot find the *lookup_value*, it finds the largest value less than the *lookup_value*. If *lookup_value* is smaller than the smallest value in the row or column being examined, the message #N/A is returned. The value returned is taken from the last row or column in the array that matches the *lookup_value*. The row or column being examined for the *lookup_value* must be sorted in ascending order.

You Supply: *lookup_value* as a number, text, name, or logical value that you are searching for; and *array* as a range of cells that contain numbers, text, names, or logical values that you compare with *lookup_value*.

Result is: a value from a one-row or one-column range, or from an array.

Match Position

Syntax: =**MATCH(***lookup_value,lookup_array, match_type***)** The MATCH function returns the position of the match for *lookup_value* in the *lookup_array*. The type of match is determined by *match_type*. The *lookup_value* can be a number, text, logical value, or cell reference. MATCH returns the row or column position in the array of the found item, not its value or cell reference.

When combined with the INDEX function, the MATCH function enables you to find exact matches to a *lookup_value* or return an error. This prevents the possible use of an incorrect value returned by VLOOKUP, HLOOKUP, or LOOKUP. The types of matches are listed in the following table, with a description of what each match type finds.

Available Match Types

Match_type	Finds
1, or omitted	Largest value less than or equal to *lookup_value*. The *lookup_array* must be in sorted order. The default is 1 if *match_type* is omitted.
0	First value that is an exact match.
–1	Smallest value greater than or equal to *lookup_value*. The *lookup_array* must be in sorted order.

You Supply: *lookup_value* as the value you use to find the value you want in a array; *lookup_array* as a range of cells containing possible lookup values, an array of values, or a reference to an array; and (optional) *match_type* as the number 1, 0, or –1, indicating which value to return (see above table).

Result is: the position of the match for *lookup_value* in the *lookup_array.*

Offset Reference

Syntax: =OFFSET(*reference,rows,cols,height,width*)

Returns the cell reference "offset" from a reference by a number of rows and a number of columns. The reference used is the *reference* argument. The reference may be a single cell or a range. The height and width of an offset range can be controlled by the *height* and *width* values. If *height* and *width* are omitted, OFFSET uses the height and width of the *reference.*

Use OFFSET to retrieve data from a table of information. Use OFFSET with the SELECTION and FORMULA functions in Excel macros to select ranges or to enter values on worksheets. Using OFFSET to specify the cell to act on is much faster than concatenating text references.

NOTE If the offset extends beyond the edge of the worksheet, or if the row or height is less than one, the OFFSET function returns #REF! ■

You Supply: *reference* as a reference to a cell or range on which you want to base the offset; *rows* as the number of rows that you want the upper-left cell of the result to refer to; *cols* as the number of columns that you want the upper-left cell of the result to refer to; (optional) *height* as the height in number of rows that you want the result to be; and (optional) *width* as the width in number of columns that you want the result to be.

Result is: a reference to a range that is a specified number of rows and columns from a cell or range.

Example: The following formula returns the value stored in cell E9:

```
=OFFSET(B7,2,3)
```

Row Number

Syntax: =**ROW**(*reference*) The ROW function results in the row number of the *reference* cell. If *reference* is a range, ROW produces a vertical array of the row numbers. If you don't specify the *reference* argument, ROW produces the row number of the cell in which the function is entered. Use the INDEX function to extract a row number as a specific element within ROW.

You Supply: *reference* as the cell or range for which you want the row number.

Result is: the row number of the *reference*.

Examples: The following formula returns 12:

```
=ROW(A12)
```

Transpose

Syntax: **=TRANSPOSE(*array*)** The TRANSPOSE function transposes the current *array* so that the first row in the current *array* becomes the first column of the new array, the second row of the current *array* becomes the second column of the new array, and so on. Because the TRANSPOSE function produces an array as a result, you must enter the TRANSPOSE function as an array formula.

You Supply: *array* as a range of cells or array of values.

Result is: a vertical range of cells as a horizontal range, or a horizontal range of cells as a vertical range.

Vertical Lookup

Syntax: **=VLOOKUP(*lookup_value,table_array, col_index_num,range_lookup*)**
The VLOOKUP function looks down the left column of *table_array* until the *lookup_value* is met, and then looks across that row to the column specified by *col_index_num*. Values in the first column can be text, numbers, or logical values in ascending order. Upper- and lowercase text are considered the same. *Range_lookup* is a logical value (TRUE or FALSE). If the value is TRUE or omitted, VLOOKUP will return an approximate match; if FALSE, VLOOKUP will return an exact match or #N/A if no match is found. If VLOOKUP cannot find *lookup_value,* the function searches for the next largest value in the first column.

You Supply: *lookup_value* as a value, reference, or text string from the first column of the table; *table_array* as a reference to the table range; *col_index_num* as the column number in the table for the value you are looking up; and (optional) *range_lookup* as a logical value of TRUE or FALSE.

Result is: the value in the same row as *lookup_value* in a table, based on the column you specify; or #N/A if no match is found.

Math and Trigonometry Functions

Many of the functions you use in worksheet calculations fall in the math and trigonometry functions category. In addition to commonly used functions such as SUM and ROUND, this category also includes more complex scientific and engineering functions.

NOTE Trigonometric functions use angles measured in radians. Use the following equations to convert between radians and degrees:

```
Radians = Degrees*p/180
Degrees = Radians*180/p
```

Absolute Value

Syntax: =**ABS(*number*)**   The ABS function returns the absolute (positive) value of the *number.*

You Supply: *number* as the number for which you want the absolute value, or a reference to a cell containing *number.*

Result is: the absolute value of the *number* (the number without its sign).

Example: The following formula returns 18 when cell A10 contains –18:

```
=ABS(A10)
```

Arccosine

Syntax: =**ACOS(*number*)**   The ACOS function produces the arccosine of the *number* in radians. ACOS is the inverse of the COS function. The *number* must be in the range –1 to 1. The resulting angle is in the range 0 to π radians (0 to 180 degrees).

You Supply: *number* as the cosine of the angle you want, between –1 and 1.

Result is: the arccosine of a *number,* in radians.

Example: The following formula returns 1.047198 (radians):

```
=ACOS(0.5)
```

Arcsine

Syntax: **=ASIN(*number*)**   The ASIN function produces the arcsine of the *number* in radians. When given a *number*, the result of a sine function, ASIN, produces the original angle measured in radians. The *number* must be in the range –1 to 1. The resulting angle will be in the range $-\pi/2$ to $\pi/2$ radians (–90 to 90 degrees).

You Supply: *number* as the sine of the angle you want, between –1 and 1.

Result is: the arcsine of a *number*, in radians.

Example: The following formula returns .523599 (radians):

```
=ASIN(0.5)
```

Arctangent

Syntax: **=ATAN(*number*)**   The ATAN function produces the arctangent of the *number* as a radian angle. ATAN is the inverse of the TAN function. The resulting angle will be in the range $-\pi/2$ to $\pi/2$ radians (–90 to 90 degrees).

You Supply: *number* as the tangent of the angle you want.

Result is: the arctangent of a *number*, in radians.

Arctangent2

Syntax: **=ATAN2(*x_number,y_number*)**   The ATAN2 function produces the arctangent for coordinate values of *x_number* and *y_number*. The resulting angle is in the range $-\pi$ to π radians (–180 to 180 degrees) excluding $-\pi$ (–180 degrees). If *x_number* and *y_number* are both 0, the function produces the message #DIV/0!.

You Supply: *x_number* as the x-coordinate of the point; and *y_number* as the y-coordinate of the point.

Result is: the arctangent of *x_number* and *y_number*, in radians.

Combination

Syntax: **=COMBIN(*number,number_chosen*)**   The COMBIN function produces the combination of items without regard to order. For example, if there are 15 socks in a drawer and you pull out two socks, there are =COMBIN(15,2) different combinations you could choose from (the answer is 105).

You Supply: *number* as the total number of items; and *number_chosen* as the number of items you choose.

Result is: the number of possible combinations for a given number of items.

Cosine
Syntax: **=COS(*number*)**   The COS function produces the cosine of the radian angle *number*.

You Supply: *number* as the angle in radians.

Result is: the cosine of the angle.

Degrees
Syntax: **=DEGREES(*angle*)**   The DEGREES function converts radians to degrees.

You Supply: *angle* as the angle in radians that you want to convert.

Result is: the number of degrees in the specified *angle*.

Even Integer
Syntax: **=EVEN(*number*)**   The EVEN function rounds a number up to an even *number*. Negative numbers are rounded away from zero.

You Supply: *number* as the value you want to round to an even number.

Result is: the number rounded up to the nearest even integer.

Example: The following formula returns 12:

```
=EVEN(10.6)
```

Exponent
Syntax: **=EXP(*number*)**   The EXP function returns e, the base of the natural logarithm, raised to the power of *number*. EXP is the inverse of the LN function. The value of e is 2.71828182845904.

You Supply: *number* as the exponent applied to the base e.

Result is: e raised to the power of the specified *number.*

Example: The following formula returns 2.718282:

```
=EXP(1)
```

Factorial

Syntax: **=FACT(*number*)** The FACT function returns the factorial of the *number,* which must be a positive number. A noninteger *number* is truncated.

You Supply: *number* as the number you want the factorial of.

Result is: the factorial of the *number.*

Examples: The following formula returns 120 (1*2*3*4*5):

```
=FACT(5)
```

The following formula returns 6 (1*2*3):

```
=FACT(3.7)
```

Integer

Syntax: **=INT(*number*)** The INT function rounds the *number* down, to the nearest integer. Negative numbers are rounded away from zero.

NOTE Use INT to round a *number* down to the nearest integer. Use TRUNC to truncate a *number* by removing the decimal portion, to a specified number of digits. Use ROUND to round a *number* to a specific number of places to the left or right of the decimal. ■

You Supply: *number* as the number you want to round down to an integer.

Result is: the number rounded down to the nearest integer.

Examples: The following formula returns 9:

```
=INT(9.6)
```

The following formula returns -10:

```
=INT(-9.6)
```

Logarithm

Syntax: =**LOG**(*number,base*)   The LOG function returns the logarithm of the *number* in the *base* specified. The value of the *number* must be positive. LOG uses base 10 if the *base* argument is omitted.

You Supply: *number* as the positive number for which you want the logarithm; and (optional) *base* as the base of the logarithm.

Result is: the logarithm of a *number,* to the *base* you specify.

Example: The following formula returns 2.26186:

    =LOG(12,3)

Mathematical Pi

Syntax: =**PI**( )   The PI function returns the value of π. An estimate of π, 3.14159265358979, is used. The parentheses must be included even though the function does not take an argument.

You Supply: only the function name followed by empty parentheses. The PI function uses no arguments.

Result is: the value of π. The number of decimals displayed on-screen depends on the column width, although all decimals in π are used in calculations.

Modulus

Syntax: =**MOD**(*number,divisor*)   The MOD function produces the remainder (modulus), of the *number* divided by the *divisor*. The #DIV/0! error appears if the *divisor* is zero.

You Supply: *number* as the number for which you want to find a remainder after the division operation; and *divisor* as the number by which you want to divide *number.*

Result is: the remainder, after a *number* is divided by the *divisor.*

Example: The following formula returns 2:

    =MOD(27,5)

Natural Log

Syntax: **=LN(*number*)** The LN function returns the natural log of the *number* in base e. LN is the inverse of the EXP function. The value of the *number* must be positive.

You Supply: *number* as the positive number for which you want the natural logarithm.

Result is: the natural logarithm of the *number.*

Example: The following formula returns 1.252763:

```
=LN(3.5)
```

Odd Integer

Syntax: **=ODD(*number*)** The ODD function produces a *number* rounded up to the closest odd number.

You Supply: *number* as the value you want to round up to an odd number.

Result is: the *number* rounded up to the nearest odd integer.

Example: The following formula returns 75:

```
=ODD(73.5)
```

Product

Syntax: **=PRODUCT(*number1,number2,...*)** The PRODUCT function multiplies *number1* by *number2* by the rest of the arguments. You can specify up to 30 arguments. Arguments that are blank cells, logical values, error values, or text are ignored. Text that can be converted into a numeric value is converted.

You Supply: *number1* as the first number that you want to multiply; (optional) *number2* as the second number you want to multiply; and so on up to 30 numbers maximum.

Result is: the product of all the *numbers* supplied as arguments.

Example: The following formula returns 24 when cells A1:A4 contain the numbers 1, 2, 3, and 4:

```
=PRODUCT(A1:A4)
```

Radians

Syntax: **=RADIANS(*angle*)** The RADIANS function converts degrees to radians.

You Supply: *angle* as an angle in degrees that you want to convert.

Result is: the radian of the specified *angle*.

Random Number

Syntax: **=RAND( )** The RAND function produces a random decimal number from 0 to 1. The function does not take an argument between the parentheses. To produce a new random number, press F9 to recalculate the formula. To freeze a random number, copy it with Edit, Copy and paste it in the same cell (using Edit, Paste Special, with the Paste Values and Operations None options). If you receive an error message when you try to use this function, run the Setup program to install the Analysis ToolPak. After you install the Analysis ToolPak, choose Tools, Add-Ins to enable this feature.

TIP To produce a random number between 0 and a number greater than 1, enter a formula that multiplies that number by the result of the RAND function. To find a random number between 0 and 100 if the RAND function is in cell B5, for example, use the formula =100*B5.

NOTE You can use the RANDBETWEEN function to find a random number between any two numbers. To find a random number between 20 and 50, for example, use the formula =RANDBETWEEN(20,50). ▪

You Supply: only the function name followed by empty parentheses. The RAND function uses no arguments.

Result is: a random number between 0 and 1.

Round Number

Syntax: **=ROUND(*number,num_digits*)** The ROUND function rounds the *number* to the number of digits specified in *num_digits*. If *num_digits* is positive, the number rounds to the specified decimal places to the right of the decimal point. If *num_digits* is zero, the number rounds to the nearest integer. If *num_digits* is negative, the number rounds to the left of the decimal point.

NOTE Use ROUND to round a *number* to a specific number of places to the left or right of the decimal. Use INT to round a *number* down to the nearest integer. Use TRUNC to truncate a *number* by removing the decimal portion, to a specified number of digits. ■

You Supply: *number* as the number you want to round; and *num_digits* as the number of digits to which you want to round.

Result is: a number rounded to the specified number of digits.

Examples: The following formula returns 102.93:

    =ROUND(102.927,2)

The following formula returns 103:

    =ROUND(102.927,0)

The following formula returns 100:

    =ROUND(102.927,-2)

Sine

Syntax: **=SIN(*number*)** The SIN function produces the sine of the radian angle *number*.

You Supply: *number* as the angle in radians for which you want the sine.

Result is: the sine of an angle.

Square Root

Syntax: **=SQRT(*number*)** The SQRT function returns the square root of the *number*. The value of the *number* must be positive.

You Supply: *number* as the positive number for which you want a square root.

Result is: the square root of *number.*

Example: The following formula returns 7.937254:

    =SQRT(63)

Sum

Syntax: =SUM(*number1,number2,...*) The SUM function calculates the sum of the arguments. Arguments can be individual values or ranges and are limited to 30 arguments. Arguments that cannot be converted from text to numbers or error values are ignored.

TIP Use the AutoSum button in the Standard toolbar to automatically sum the numbers in an adjacent range. Excel supplies a suggested range of numbers to sum; if the range is incorrect, drag in the worksheet to indicate the correct range and then press Enter.

You Supply: *number1* as the first number, cell, or range you want to sum; (optional) *number2* as the second number, cell, or range you want to sum; and so on up to 30 arguments maximum.

Result is: the sum of the supplied arguments.

Tangent

Syntax: =TAN(*number*) The TAN function produces the tangent of the radian angle *number.*

You Supply: *number* as the angle in radians for which you want the tangent.

Result is: the tangent of an angle.

Truncate Number

Syntax: =TRUNC(*number,num_digits*) The TRUNC function changes the *number* to an integer by cutting off, or truncating, the decimal fraction portion. If *num_digits* is omitted, it is assumed to be zero.

NOTE Use TRUNC to truncate a *number* by removing the decimal portion, to a specified number of digits. Use INT to round a *number* down to the nearest integer. Use ROUND to round a *number* to a specific number of places to the left or right of the decimal. ■

You Supply: *number* as the number you want to truncate; and (optional) *num_digits* as a number specifying the precision of the truncation.

Result is: the *number* truncated to the number of decimals specified.

Example: The following formula returns `5.63`:

```
=TRUNC(5.6357,2)
```

Statistical Functions

Statistical functions can help you with simple problems, such as finding an average or counting items. Statistical functions also can perform simple statistical analysis, such as finding the standard deviation and variance of a set of numbers.

Average
Syntax: **=AVERAGE(*number1*,*number2*,...)** The AVER-AGE function returns the average (mean) of the arguments. Arguments may be single values, cells, or ranges. The ranges can contain numbers, cell references, or arrays that contain numbers. Text, logical values, errors, and blank cells are ignored. AVERAGE can take from 1 to 30 arguments.

You Supply: *number1* as the first number or range you want to average; (optional) *number2* as the second number or range you want to include in the average; and so on up to 30 arguments maximum.

Result is: the average, or arithmetic mean, of the supplied arguments.

Conditional Count
Syntax: **=COUNTIF(*range*,*criteria*)** The COUNTIF function counts the number of cells within *range* that match *criteria*.

Only nonblank cells are included in the count. The *criteria* argument can be a number, text, or an expression. If *criteria* is not just a number, you must enclose it within quotation marks.

You Supply: *range* as the range of cells you want to count; and *criteria* as the condition that defines which cells you want to count.

Result is: the number of cells in the *range* that meet the specified *criteria*.

Example: The following formula returns 1 if the range B1:B4 contains the numbers 57, 102, 84, and 98:

```
=COUNTIF(B1:B4,">100")
```

Count
Syntax: =COUNT(*value1,value2,...*)   The COUNT function produces a count of the numbers in the arguments. The *value* arguments can be numbers, cell references, or arrays that contain numbers. Text, logical values, errors, and blank cells are not counted. You can include from 1 to 30 arguments in COUNT.

NOTE   Although the arguments in the COUNT function can reference ranges that include both numbers and text, only the numbers are actually counted. ■

You Supply: *value1* as the first number or range you want to count; *value2* as the second number or range you want to include in the count; and so on up to 30 arguments maximum.

Result is: the total count of the numbers in the supplied arguments.

Maximum Value
Syntax: =MAX(*number1,number2,...*)   The MAX function produces the largest value among the arguments. MAX can take up to 30 arguments. Arguments that are error values or text that cannot be interpreted as a number are ignored. Within a referenced array or range, any empty cells, logical values, text, or error values are ignored.

FUNCTIONS MINI-REFERENCE

You Supply: *number1* as the first number or range for which you want the maximum number; (optional) *number2* as the second number or range for which you want the maximum number; and so on up to 30 arguments maximum.

Result is: the largest value in the supplied arguments.

Median Value

Syntax: =MEDIAN(*number1,number2,...*) The MEDIAN function returns the median value of the arguments. The median value is the middle value in a set of numbers. MEDIAN can take up to 30 arguments. If MEDIAN includes an even number of arguments, then MEDIAN calculates the average of the two middle values.

You Supply: *number1* as the first number or range for which you want the median value; (optional) *number2* as the second number or range for which you want the median value; and so on up to 30 arguments maximum.

Result is: the median (middle) value of the supplied arguments.

Examples: The following formula returns 4:

```
=MEDIAN(1,4,2,6,9)
```

The following formula returns 5 (the average of the two middle values, 4 and 6):

```
=MEDIAN(1,4,2,6,9,10)
```

Minimum Value

Syntax: =MIN(*number1,number2,...*) The MIN function produces the smallest value among the arguments. MIN can take up to 30 arguments. Arguments that are not numbers are ignored. If the arguments contain no numbers, MIN produces 0.

You Supply: *number1* as the first number or range for which you want the minimum value; (optional) *number2* as the second number or range for which you want the minimum value; and so on up to 30 arguments maximum.

Result is: the smallest value in the supplied arguments.

Standard Deviation (Entire Population)

Syntax: =**STDEVP(***number1,number2,...***)** The STDEVP function calculates the standard deviation of a population, where the entire population is listed in the arguments. STDEV can take up to 30 arguments. If the arguments do not include the entire population, use STDEV instead. (See also the "Standard Deviation (Sample Population)" function.)

You Supply: *number1* as the first number or reference to include in the population; (optional) *number2* as the second number or reference to include in the population; and so on up to 30 arguments maximum.

Result is: the standard deviation based on all values in the population.

Standard Deviation (Sample Population)

Syntax: =**STDEV(***number1,number2,...***)** The STDEV function calculates an estimate of the standard deviation of a population, based on a sample of the population. STDEV can take up to 30 arguments. If the arguments include the entire population, use STDEVP instead. (See also the "Standard Deviation (Entire Population)" function.)

You Supply: *number1* as the first number or reference to include in the sample; (optional) *number2* as the second number or reference to include in the sample; and so on up to 30 arguments maximum.

Result is: the standard deviation based on a sample of values in the population.

Variance (Entire Population)

Syntax: =**VARP(***number1,number2,...***)** The VARP function calculates the variance of a population, where the entire population is listed in the arguments. Use VAR instead if the arguments contain only a sample of the population. (See also the "Variance (Sample Population)" function.)

You Supply: *number1* as the first number or reference to include in the population; (optional) *number2* as the second number or reference to include in the population; and so on up to 30 arguments maximum.

Result is: the variance based on all values in the population.

Variance (Sample Population)

Syntax: =VAR(***number1***,*number2*,...)   The VAR function calculates an estimate of the variance in a population, based on a sample of the population. Use VARP if the arguments contain the entire population. (See also the "Variance (Entire Population)" function.)

You Supply: *number1* as the first number or reference to include in the sample; (optional) *number2* as the second number or reference to include in the sample; and so on up to 30 arguments maximum.

Result is: the variance based on a sample of values in the population.

Text Functions

The text functions enable you to manipulate text strings. You can extract portions of text from long strings of text, or you can change numbers and dates to text so that they can exceed a cell's width without producing a cell filled with #####. Numbers or dates converted to text can be joined to text in titles, sentences, and labels. Text functions are also useful for manipulating text that you want to convert to ASCII files.

ASCII Character

Syntax: =CHAR(***number***)   The CHAR function produces the character corresponding to the ASCII code *number* between 1 and 255.

You Supply: *number* a number between 1 and 255 specifying the character you want.

Result is: the character specified by the code number, based on the character set that your computer uses.

ASCII Code

Syntax: =CODE(*text*) The CODE function produces the ASCII code of the first letter in the specified *text*.

You Supply: *text* as the text for which you want the code of the first character.

Result is: a numeric code for the first character in a text string, based on the character set that your computer uses.

Clean Text

Syntax: =CLEAN(*text*) The CLEAN function removes from the specified *text* argument any characters that are lower than ASCII 32 or above ASCII 127. These characters are not printed. This function is useful for removing control codes, bells, and non-ASCII characters from imported text.

You Supply: *text* as the text string that you want to clean.

Result is: the *text* string excluding all nonprintable characters.

Concatenate Text

Syntax: =CONCATENATE(*text1*,*text2*,...) The CONCAT-ENATE function joins *text1* to *text2*. CONCATENATE can take up to 30 arguments. The arguments can include text strings, numbers, or single-cell references.

You Supply: *text1* as the first text string you want to join into a single text string; (optional) *text2* as the second text string you want to join into a single text string; and so on up to 30 arguments maximum.

Result is: a single text string that joins all the text strings supplied as arguments.

Example: You can use the CONCATENATE function to join text strings in an address database. For example, the following formula returns Anne M. Miller if cell A3 contains Anne, cell B3 contains M. and cell C3 contains Miller:

```
=CONCATENATE(A3," ",B3," ",C3)
```

Note that the second and fourth arguments in the above example are used to insert a single space between the first name and middle initial, and between the middle initial and last name.

Convert Text

Syntax: =**TEXT(*value, format_text*)** The TEXT function converts the numeric *value* to text and displays it with the format specified by *format_text*. The result appears to be a formatted number, but actually is text. Use one of the pre-defined or custom numeric formats to specify the format for the *value*. The format cannot contain an asterisk (*), nor can it be in the General format.

You Supply: *value* as a number or cell reference; and *format_text* as a number format in text form, from the Category box on the Number tab of the Format Cells dialog box (other than General format).

Result is: a value converted to text in the specified number format.

Example: The following formula returns $1,234.56:

```
=TEXT(1234.56,"$#,##0.00")
```

Exact Comparison

Syntax: =**EXACT(*text1,text2*)** The EXACT function compares the *text1* and *text2* arguments. If they are exactly the same, EXACT returns the logical TRUE; if they are not the same, EXACT returns FALSE. Upper- and lowercase text are considered to be different in the arguments.

You Supply: *text1* as the first text string; and *text2* as the second text string you want to compare.

Result is: TRUE if the arguments match exactly, or FALSE if they don't match.

Find Text

Syntax: =**FIND(*find_text,within_text,start_num*)**
Beginning at *start_num,* the FIND function searches the text specified by *within_text* to locate *find_text*. If *find_text* is found, the FIND function produces the character location where

find_text starts. If *start_num* is out of limits or a match is not found, the #VALUE! error value is displayed. If *start_num* is not specified, it is assumed to be 1, which is the starting character. Unlike the SEARCH function, FIND is case-sensitive and doesn't allow wildcard characters.

You Supply: *find_text* as the text you want to find; *within_text* as the text containing the text you want to find; and (optional) *start_num* as the character position in which you want to start the search.

Result is: the number of the starting position of the found string.

Example: The following formula returns 4 if cell C5 contains X:

```
=FIND(C5,"123XYZ")
```

Fixed Decimals

Syntax: **=FIXED**(*number,decimals,no_commas*)   The FIXED function rounds the *number* to the specified *decimals* and displays it as text in fixed decimal format with commas. If you omit *decimals,* the *number* is rounded to two decimal places. If you specify a negative number of *decimals,* the function rounds the *number* to the left of the decimal point. When *no_commas* is TRUE, commas are removed from the result. If you omit *no_commas,* commas are displayed in the result.

You Supply: *number* as the number you want to round and convert to text; (optional) *decimals* as the number of digits to the right of the decimal point; and (optional) *no_commas* as TRUE if you don't want to display commas in the result, or FALSE if you do want to display commas.

Result is: a number rounded to the specified number of decimal points, either with or without commas (as indicated by the *no_commas* argument).

Examples: The following formula returns 1,234.57:

```
=FIXED(1234.567)
```

The following formula returns 1200:

```
=FIXED(1234.567,-2,TRUE)
```

Leftmost Characters

Syntax: =**LEFT**(*text,num_chars*)   The LEFT function produces the leftmost number of characters from *text*. The value of *num_chars* must be greater than zero. If *num_chars* is omitted, it is assumed to be 1.

You Supply: *text* as the text string containing the character(s) you want to extract; and (optional) *num_chars* as the number of characters you want to extract.

Result is: the specified number of leftmost character(s) in the text string.

Example: The following formula returns 3rd if cell E20 contains 3rd Edition:

```
=LEFT(E20,3)
```

Lowercase Text

Syntax: =**LOWER**(*text*)   The LOWER function changes all *text* in the argument to lowercase.

You Supply: *text* as the text string you want to convert to lowercase.

Result is: the text string with all letters in lowercase.

Example: The following formula returns part number bx154c when cell B7 contains Part Number BX154C:

```
=LOWER(B7)
```

Middle Characters

Syntax: =**MID**(*text,start_num,num_chars*)   The MID function produces characters from the specified *text,* beginning at the character in the *start_num* position and extending the specified *num_chars*.

You Supply: *text* as the text string containing the character(s) you want to extract; *start_num* as the position of the first character you want to extract (the first character in *text* is number

1); and *num_chars* as the number of characters you want to extract.

Result is: the specified number of characters from a text string, starting at the position you specify.

Example: The following formula returns BX512A:

```
=MID("Part number BX512A is not available",13,6)
```

Proper Text

Syntax: =PROPER(*text*) The PROPER function changes *text* in the argument to lowercase with initial capitals for each word.

You Supply: *text* as the text string you want to convert to proper text.

Result is: the text string with the first letter in each word capitalized.

Repeat Text

Syntax: =REPT(*text,number_times*) The REPT function repeats the *text* for *number_times*. The value of *number_times* must be positive and nonzero. The maximum number of resulting characters is 255.

You Supply: *text* as the text you want to repeat; and *number_times* as the number of times you want to repeat *text*.

Result is: the *text* string repeated the number of times specified.

Example: The following formula returns #___#___#___ as the text string:

```
=REPT("#___",3)
```

Replace Text

Syntax: =REPLACE(*old_text,start_num,num_chars, new_text*)
The REPLACE function replaces the characters in *old_text* with *new_text,* starting with the character at *start_num* and continuing for the specified *num_chars*. The first character in *old_text* is character 1. (See also the "Substitute Text" function.)

You Supply: *old_text* as the text string in which you want to replace characters; *start_num* as the first character position in *old_text* that you want to replace with *new_text*; *num_chars* as the number of characters in *old_text* that you want to replace; and *new_text* as the text that will replace characters in *old_text*.

Result is: the text string with *old_text* replaced by *new_text*.

Example: The following formula returns Year: 2000 as the text string:

```
=REPLACE("Year: 1999",7,4,"2000")
```

Rightmost Characters

Syntax: =**RIGHT(***text,num_chars***)** The RIGHT function produces the rightmost number of characters from *text*. The value of *num_chars* must be greater than zero. If *num_chars* is omitted, it is assumed to be 1.

You Supply: *text* as the text string containing the character(s) you want to extract; and (optional) *num_chars* as the number of characters you want to extract.

Result is: the specified number of rightmost character(s) in the text string.

Example: The following formula returns IN as the text string:

```
=RIGHT("Indianapolis, IN",2)
```

Search Text

Syntax: =**SEARCH(***find_text,within_text,start_num***)** The SEARCH function begins at *start_num* in the specified *within_text* argument, searches through it for *find_text,* and produces the character number where *find_text* begins. The first character position in *within_text* is 1. If *start_num* is omitted, it is assumed to be 1. SEARCH ignores case differences. If *find_text* is not found or if *start_num* is out of limits, #VALUE! is returned.

The wild card ? can be used in *find_text* to specify any single character at that location within the text you want to find. The wild card * can be used in *find_text* to specify any group of characters at that location within the text you want to find. SEARCH is not case-sensitive (unlike the FIND function).

You Supply: *find_text* as the text you want to find; *within_text* as the text containing the text you want to find; and (optional) *start_num* as the character position in which you want to start the search.

Result is: the number of the starting position of the found string.

Example: The following formula returns 13:

```
=SEARCH("BX*","Part number BX512A is not available")
```

Substitute Text

Syntax: **=SUBSTITUTE(***text,old_text,new_text, instance_num***)** The SUBSTITUTE function substitutes *new_text* for *old_text* within the specified *text*. If *old_text* occurs more than once, *instance_num* specifies which occurrence to replace. If *instance_num* is not specified, every occurrence of *old_text* is replaced. SUBSTITUTE is case-sensitive. If you want to replace specific text in a text string, use SUBSTITUTE. If you want to replace any text that occurs in a specific location in a text string, use the REPLACE function. (See also the "REPLACE" function.)

You Supply: *text* as the text in which you want to substitute characters; *old_text* as the text you want to replace; *new_text* as the text that will replace *old_text*; and (optional) *instance_num* as a number indicating which occurrence of *old_text* you want to replace.

Result is: the text string with *old_text* replaced by *new_text* at the specified occurrence (or all occurrences if *instance_num* is omitted).

Text Value

Syntax: **=T(***value***)** The T function returns text when *value* is text, or double quotes (empty text) when *value* is not text.

You Supply: *value* as the value you want to test.

Result is: the text referred to by *value,* or empty text if *value* is not text.

Trim Text

Syntax: **=TRIM(*text*)** The TRIM function deletes all spaces from *text* so that only one space remains between words. This can be useful for cleaning text used in databases, or text imported to or exported from Excel.

You Supply: *text* as the text string from which you want excess spaces removed.

Result is: the text string with all spaces removed (except for one space between words).

Uppercase Text

Syntax: **=UPPER(*text*)** The UPPER function changes all *text* in the argument to uppercase.

You Supply: *text* as the text string you want to convert to uppercase.

Result is: the text string with all letters in uppercase.

Example: The following formula returns PART NUMBER BX154C when cell B7 contains Part Number BX154C:

```
=UPPER(B7)
```

Glossary

This glossary contains the terms that appear italicized throughout this book. Look them up as you go along or scan for any terms with which you are not familiar.

A

absolute reference　A cell reference in a formula that doesn't change when you copy that formula to another cell or range. You use dollar signs to indicate absolute references, such as B7.

alignment　How a cell entry is positioned in a cell, both horizontally and vertically.

arguments　Inputs used to calculate functions.

AutoCalculate　An Excel feature that supplies a quick total in a worksheet.

AutoComplete　An Excel feature that makes it easy to enter repeated text items in a column.

AutoCorrect　An Excel feature that automatically corrects common typographical or spelling errors as you type them.

AutoFill　An Excel feature that enables you to enter sequences of values automatically.

AutoFilter　An Excel feature that enables you to filter data in a list without moving or sorting the list. The field names at the top of the list become drop-down lists from which you can choose the data you want to view.

AutoFormat   An Excel feature that applies a set of pre-defined formatting choices to reports, tables, and lists.

AutoShapes   Ready-made shapes provided with Excel (such as stars and flowchart symbols) that you can add to worksheets.

AutoSum   An Excel feature that enables you to sum adjacent columns or rows automatically.

C

chart   A graphical representation of data in an Excel worksheet.

Chart Wizard   An Excel feature that automates the creation of a chart.

clip art   A collection of graphics and pictures that is available for use in programs such as Excel.

Clipboard   A temporary storage area for cut or copied items in Windows applications.

concatenation   Combining text, numbers, or dates within a single cell. In Excel, you use the ampersand (&) symbol to join the contents of multiple cells.

controls   Data-entry objects commonly used in Excel forms, such as scrolling lists or check boxes.

D

database   In Excel, information that contains similar sets of data, organized in *records* and *fields*.

data form   A dialog box which enables you to quickly insert records in a list or database, as well as search for and delete existing records.

data labels Identifiers that you can attach to data points on a chart.

data mapping An Excel feature that enables you to see the relationships between numbers and geographic features.

dependents Cells that contain formulas that refer to other cells.

F

field The information in one column of a list or database.

form An organized and formatted worksheet that facilitates data entry.

formula Calculations you enter in a worksheet.

formula palette A pop-up window that appears under the Formula bar when you use Paste Function to enter a formula or function.

function A predefined formula that performs a specific operation in Excel.

G

Goal Seek An Excel feature that produces a specific value in a formula cell by adjusting one input cell that influences a value.

H

hyperlink A link in an Excel workbook that enables you to quickly jump to Internet or intranet sites, or to other Excel workbooks or Office documents.

L

legend   A chart or map element that explains the markers or symbols used in a chart.

list   See *database*.

M

macro   A stored list of commands and keystrokes that are automatically executed by Excel.

mixed reference   A cell reference in a formula in which only the row number or column letter (but not both) remains fixed when you copy that formula to another cell or range.

O

Object Linking and Embedding (OLE)   A Windows feature that enables you to create work in one application and share that work with another application.

Office Assistant   An on-screen, interactive program that provides tips and Help information, and also interprets what Help you might need based on your current actions.

orientation   How a cell entry or chart object is positioned in a cell or chart, rotating between –90 and 90 degrees. Also refers to how text is printed on a page—across the short edge of the page (portrait) or across the long edge of the page (landscape).

outlining   An Excel feature that enables you to expand or contract information contained in worksheets or reports so that you see more or less detail.

P

Paste Function   An Excel feature that automates the process of entering a function.

pivot table   A feature that enables you to summarize and analyze data in lists and tables. Pivot tables are called such because you can quickly rearrange the position of pivot table fields to give you a different view of the table.

PivotTable Wizard   An Excel feature that automates the creation of a pivot table.

precedents   Cells that are referred to by a formula.

R

record   The information in one row of a list or database.

relative reference   A cell reference in a formula that automatically adjusts when you copy that formula to another cell or range.

S

ScreenTips   The small pop-up labels that appear next to a toolbar button when you move the mouse pointer onto the button and pause.

serial number   The value used to store a date or time in Excel. Days are numbered from the beginning of the century—the date serial number 1 corresponds to the date January 1, 1900. Time serial numbers are stored as a decimal fraction.

sheet   See *worksheet*.

Solver   An Excel add-in program that finds an optimal solution by adjusting input cells, while ensuring that other formulas in the worksheet stay within specified limits.

T

Template Wizard   An Excel feature that enables you to quickly create professional-looking data entry forms.

tracer lines   Lines showing the flow of data through the worksheet by connecting the active cell with related cells; used with the Excel auditing feature.

W

workbook   The Excel file in which you work and store data. A workbook can contain one or more sheets of varying types: worksheets, chart sheets, MS Excel 4.0 Macro sheets, and MS Excel 5.0 Dialog sheets.

worksheet   The document you use in Excel to enter and edit data (also sometimes referred to as a sheet).

worksheet frame   The column and row headings that appear in the workbook window.

workspace   A collection of open workbooks that Excel can save and then redisplay when you start the program. Excel saves information such as the workbook names, screen locations, and window sizes.

Index

Complete and Return this Card
for a *FREE* Computer Book Catalog

Thank you for purchasing this book! You have purchased a superior computer book written expressly for your needs. To continue to provide the kind of up-to-date, pertinent coverage you've come to expect from us, we need to hear from you. Please take a minute to complete and return this self-addressed, postage-paid form. In return, we'll send you a free catalog of all our computer books on topics ranging from word processing to programming and the internet.

Mr. ☐   Mrs. ☐   Ms. ☐   Dr. ☐

Name (first) ☐☐☐☐☐☐☐☐☐☐ (M.I.) ☐ (last) ☐☐☐☐☐☐☐☐☐☐☐☐☐☐

Address ☐☐☐☐☐☐☐☐☐☐☐☐☐☐☐☐☐☐☐☐☐☐☐☐☐☐☐☐

☐☐☐☐☐☐☐☐☐☐☐☐☐☐☐☐☐☐☐☐☐☐☐☐☐☐☐☐

City ☐☐☐☐☐☐☐☐☐☐☐ State ☐☐ Zip ☐☐☐☐☐ ☐☐☐☐

Phone ☐☐☐ ☐☐☐ ☐☐☐☐ Fax ☐☐☐ ☐☐☐ ☐☐☐☐

Company Name ☐☐☐☐☐☐☐☐☐☐☐☐☐☐☐☐☐☐☐☐☐☐

E-mail address ☐☐☐☐☐☐☐☐☐☐☐☐☐☐☐☐☐☐☐☐☐☐☐☐☐☐☐☐☐

1. Please check at least (3) influencing factors for purchasing this book.

Front or back cover information on book .... ☐
Special approach to the content .... ☐
Completeness of content .... ☐
Author's reputation .... ☐
Publisher's reputation .... ☐
Book cover design or layout .... ☐
Index or table of contents of book .... ☐
Price of book .... ☐
Special effects, graphics, illustrations .... ☐
Other (Please specify): _____ ☐

2. How did you first learn about this book?

Internet Site .... ☐
Saw in Macmillan Computer
   Publishing catalog .... ☐
Recommended by store personnel .... ☐
Saw the book on bookshelf at store .... ☐
Recommended by a friend .... ☐
Received advertisement in the mail .... ☐
Saw an advertisement in: _____ ☐
Read book review in: _____ ☐
Other (Please specify): _____ ☐

3. How many computer books have you purchased in the last six months?

This book only .... ☐   3 to 5 books .... ☐
2 books .... ☐   More than 5 .... ☐

4. Where did you purchase this book?

Bookstore .... ☐
Computer Store .... ☐
Consumer Electronics Store .... ☐
Department Store .... ☐
Office Club .... ☐
Warehouse Club .... ☐
Mail Order .... ☐
Direct from Publisher .... ☐
Internet site .... ☐
Other (Please specify): .... ☐

5. How long have you been using a computer?

Less than 6 months .. ☐   6 months to a year ..... ☐
1 to 3 years .... ☐   More than 3 years ...... ☐

6. What is your level of experience with personal computers and with the subject of this book?

	With PC's	With subject of book
New	☐	☐
Casual	☐	☐
Accomplished	☐	☐
Expert	☐	☐

Source Code — ISBN: 0-7897-1165-6

7. Which of the following best describes your job title?

Administrative Assistant .... ☐
Coordinator .... ☐
Manager/Supervisor .... ☐
Director .... ☐
Vice President .... ☐
President/CEO/COO .... ☐
Lawyer/Doctor/Medical Professional .... ☐
Teacher/Educator/Trainer .... ☐
Engineer/Technician .... ☐
Consultant .... ☐
Not employed/Student/Retired .... ☐
Other (Please specify): .... ☐

8. Which of the following best describes the area of the company your job title falls under?

Accounting .... ☐
Engineering .... ☐
Manufacturing .... ☐
Marketing .... ☐
Operations .... ☐
Sales .... ☐
Other (Please specify): .... ☐

9. What is your age?

Under 20 .... ☐
21-29 .... ☐
30-39 .... ☐
40-49 .... ☐
50-59 .... ☐
60-over .... ☐

10. Are you:

Male .... ☐
Female .... ☐

11. Which computer publications do you read regularly? (Please list)

_____
_____
_____
_____
_____
_____
_____
_____
_____
_____

Comments: _____
_____
_____

Fold here and scotch-tape to mail.

Microsoft Excel 97 Shortcuts and Function Keys

IntelliMouse

Operation	Shortcut
Scroll up or down by row	Roll wheel forward or back
Pan across worksheet	Hold down wheel and drag
Start automatic scrolling	Click wheel button, drag and stop
Stop automatic scrolling	Click mouse button
Zoom view	Ctrl+roll wheel button
Zoom outline details	Point to cell, Shift+roll wheel button

Function Keys

Key	Function	Key	Function
F1	Help	Ctrl+F6	Next workbook
Shift+F1	What's This balloon	Ctrl+Shift+F6	Previous workbook
Alt+F1	Insert chart sheet	F7	Spelling
F2	Edit cell contents	Ctrl+F7	Move window
Shift+F2	Edit a comment	F8	Extend selection
Alt+F2	Save As command	Shift+F8	Turn on or off Add mode
F3	Paste name	Alt+F8	Display Macro dialog box
Shift+F3	Paste function	F9	Calculate all open sheets
Ctrl+F3	Define a name	Shift+F9	Calculate active sheet
Ctrl+Shift+F3	Create names using labels	Ctrl+F9	Minimize workbook
F4	Repeat last action	F10	Activate menu bar to use with cursor keys
Shift+F4	Repeat last Find	Shift+F10	Display shortcut menu
Ctrl+F4	Close document	Ctrl+F10	Maximize document
Alt+F4	Close Excel	F11	Create chart
F5	Go To	Shift+F11	Insert new worksheet
Shift+F5	Find	Ctrl+F11	Insert Excel 4 macro sheet
Ctrl+F5	Restore window	Alt+F11	Display Visual Basic Editor
F6	Next pane	F+F12	Open command
Shift+F6	Previous pane	Ctrl+Shift+F12	Print command

A (+) sign in these tables indicates that you should hold down the first key while pressing the second key, as in Alt+A. A comma (,) indicates that you should release the first key before pressing the second key, as in Alt, A.

If your keyboard has only 10 function keys, use Alt+F1 for the F11 key and Alt+F2 for the F12 key.

201 W. 103rd Street, Indianapolis, IN 46290 (317) 581-3500
Copyright© 1996 by Que® Corporation.

Microsoft Excel 97 Integration Grid

If you want to move information from Excel to another Microsoft Office application, you may find the suggestions in this grid helpful. Each numbered item under the application name represents a different option. This is not a full explanation. These are just some ideas to get you started.

Word

1. Excel: Edit, Copy range. Word: Edit, Paste items become a table.

2. Word: Edit, Paste Special—Unformatted text items become tabbed entries.

3. Word: Tools, Mail Merge, Data, Get Data, Open Data Source.

Excel

1. Type = and then move to other cell in other workbook to link one formula.

2. Edit, Copy. Edit, Paste Special, Paste Link to link a range.

Access*

1. Excel: Data, Convert to Access—new table.

2. Excel: Data, MS Access Form—creates Excel link & form.

3. Excel: Data, MS Access Report.

4. Excel: Edit, Copy. Access: Paste Append into table with same order of fields.

PowerPoint

1. Excel: Edit, Copy. PowerPoint: Edit, Paste As Hyperlink.

2. PowerPoint: Insert MS Excel Worksheet button.

3. Edit, Paste Special—Unformatted Text takes PowerPoint formatting.

4. Edit, Paste Special, Formatted Text takes Excel formatting.

Outlook

1. Word: File, Send To, Mail Recipient or Routing Recipient.

2. Outlook: File, Import and Export, Import from Schedule+ or... (named range in Excel).

3. Outlook: Contacts notes field, Insert, Object, Display As Icon.

NOTE: You may need to add the AccessLinks Add-in before you begin this procedure. Check the Excel on-line Help for instructions. If the AccessLinks Add-ins are unavailable, you may need to reinstall Microsoft Office. See appropriate Microsoft documentation for installation upgrade instructions.

General Instructions for All Products

Insert Hyperlink. Use to launch Office application and document and optionally go to specific part of document.

1. Optionally type and select text to appear as description instead of file name and path.
2. Insert, Hyperlink.
3. Enter file name or URL and location within file.

Insert Object. Embed instructions for editing source information—stored in target file. Also, link information so when source changes, target is updated.

1. Insert, Object, Create New or Create from File.